THE ALL-COLOUR
INDIAN
COOKBOOK

Recipes by Mridula Baljekar
Photography by Peter Barry
Recipes styled by Bridgeen Deery and Wendy Devenish
Designed by Philip Clucas and Claire Leighton

CLB 3436
Published in 1993 by CLB Publishing
Exclusively for Selecta Book Ltd, Devizes
© 1993 CLB Publishing
ISBN 1-85833-071-8

Printed and bound in Singapore

THE ALL-COLOUR
INDIAN
COOKBOOK

SELECT
EDITIONS

Contents

Introduction

The wonderfully diverse cuisine of India has been formed by many influences over the centuries. In this vast country, the cooking of each area has been shaped by the local climate, terrain, and population.

Invaders, in the past, brought with them their own styles of cooking and the ingredients which helped shape modern day Indian cuisine. The Mughals introduced exotic spices, and dried fruits and nuts from Afganistan which they combined with milk and coconut to create the famous 'Mughlai' cuisine. The Kashmiris contributed vegetarian dishes as well as saffron and other uncommon condiments to liven up sweetmeats and puddings. The Persians gave the 'Dhansak' style of cooking – a delicious combination of chicken or lamb cooked with lentils and spices.

Although curries are the staple of Indian cuisine, not every dish that is spicy is a curry. The word curry actually means sauce, so technically any dish that is dry is not a curry. A dry vegetable dish for example is called a 'bhaji' while a 'dum' dish, similar to a pot roast, has little or no sauce. A 'korma' is a braised dish and a 'bhoona' is a fried dish.

In India, it takes a long time to become a good cook as none of the recipes are quantified and the exact blend and measurement of all ingredients is estimated, with the recipes being handed down from one generation to the next. Fortunately for us these recipes have been tested and written down so that a perfect result can be achieved without relying on experience or guess work. One of the great advantages of Indian cookery is its versatility and relative simplicity – once familiar with the various ingredients a cook can easily adapt recipes to personal preferences.

TECHNIQUES
Spices
In India spices are usually freshly ground before cooking each meal, as this ensures the best results.

Heat a cast-iron or other heavy-based frying pan without adding any fat. Add the spices and dry-roast them gently, stirring or tossing them in the pan until they smell aromatic. Allow the spices to cool out of the pan, as the pan will retain the heat for a while and the spices could easily burn and become bitter. Grind the spices in a small electric coffee grinder which is kept solely for this purpose, or you will end up with very strange tasting coffee!

When frying ground spices it is essential to follow given times in recipes and to ensure that the fat does not overheat as the spices will burn and become bitter.

Rice

Long grain rice is generally used in Indian cooking. Basmati is the superior quality rice used in all pilaus and birianis. It differs from ordinary long grain rice in that it has matured for up to five years after harvesting. This type of rice cooks better as it won't stick. Basmati rice should be washed in cold water at least twice, then soaked for thirty minutes before stirring and draining thoroughly. This reduces the starch content and prepares the grains to absorb the moisture during cooking. If using other long grain rice wash three times and soak for an hour or so before using. It is important to remember that when rice has been cooked it is fragile and should not be stirred until it has had time to stand. Fork the rice through gently just before serving.

Salt

Salt is used in what seems like quite large quantities in Indian cooking, but this is for a very important reason. Salt subdues the flavour of spices and chillies, and without the correct amount of salt the spices become overpowering. When salt is added to some dishes, particularly vegetables, it causes them to release their juices and they can therefore be cooked without having to add extra liquid. If the amount of salt is to be drastically reduced in a recipe, it is advisable to adjust the quantity of spices too, although this will carry the risk of losing the authentic taste of the dish.

Chicken and Meat

In Indian cooking the skin is always removed from chicken to allow the spices to penetrate into the meat. It is usually cooked on the bone and in small pieces, so that the spices can flavour the whole of the meat. All fat should be trimmed off meat and it should be dried thoroughly on kitchen paper before frying, as any moisture on the meat will cause it to braise instead.

Oil and Ghee

The traditional cooking fat is ghee – the Hindi word for clarified butter – which is produced by removing the whey solids from butter when it is melted. It has a higher cooking temperature than butter and a longer shelf life, without needing refrigeration. However, since the dangers of eating too much saturated fat have become apparent, many people may prefer to use vegetable oil – although ghee is necessary for certain dishes, such as pilaus, birianis and some Mughlai dishes.

SERVING AN INDIAN MEAL

In India a meal does not comprise of starters and a main course; several dishes are brought to the table together for everyone to help themselves. A typical meal would include rice, a vegetable pulse dish, accompaniments such as a pickle or chutney and often some kind of bread, as well as at least two 'main course' dishes.

Alcohol is rarely drunk in India, where either water, fruit based drinks or tea are the norm. If you do wish to serve alcohol, lager or dry white wine are the best choices.

Chapter 1
Snacks and Starters

SEEKH KABABS

Wooden skewers about 6-8-inches long are the best type of skewers for these kababs. You can use metal or steel skewers, but allow the skewers to cool before shaping the next batch of kababs onto them.

MAKES 18 Kababs

Juice of half a lemon

2 tbsps chopped fresh mint or 1 tsp dried or bottled mint

3-4 tbsps chopped coriander leaves

25g/1oz raw cashews

1 medium-sized onion, coarsely chopped

2 small cloves of garlic, peeled and coarsely chopped

1-2 fresh green chillies, finely chopped or minced; remove the seeds if you like it mild

700g/1½lb lean mince, beef or lamb

2 tsps ground coriander

2 tsps ground cumin

1 tsp ground ajwain (ajowan or carum) or ground caraway seeds

½ tsp garam masala

½ tsp Tandoori colour or a few drops of red food colouring mixed with 1 tbsp tomato purée

½ tsp freshly ground black pepper

1 egg yolk

¼ tsp chilli powder

1 tsp salt or to taste

4 tbsps cooking oil

Grind the following ingredients in a coffee grinder

2 tbsps white poppy seeds

2 tbsps sesame seeds

1. Put the lemon juice, mint, coriander leaves, cashews, onion, garlic and green chillies in an electric liquidiser and blend to a smooth paste. Transfer the mixture to a large bowl.

2. Using the liquidiser, grind the mince in 2-3 small batches until it is fairly smooth, rather like a paste. Add the meat to the rest of the liquidised ingredients in the bowl.

3. Add the rest of the ingredients, except the the oil and knead the mixture until all the ingredients are mixed thoroughly and it is smooth. Alternatively, put all the ingredients, except the oil, in an electric food processor and process until the mixture is smooth.

4. Chill the mixture for 30 minutes.

5. Preheat oven to 240°C/475°F, Gas Mark 9. Line a roasting tin with aluminium foil.

6. Divide the kabab mix into about 18 balls, each slightly larger than a golf ball.

7. Mould a ball onto a skewer and form into a sausage shape by gently rolling between your palms (about 4-5-inches long) and place on the prepared roasting tin. Make the rest of the kababs the same way.

8. Brush generously with the oil and place the roasting tin just below the top rung of the oven. Cook for 6-8 minutes. Remove the tin from the oven and brush the kababs liberally with the remaining oil and cook for a further 6-8 minutes.

9. Allow the kababs to cool slightly before removing them from the skewers.

TIME Preparation takes 15-20 minutes, cooking takes 35-40 minutes.

ONION BHAJIYAS

Onion Bhajiyas are popular all over India and have established themselves as a firm favourite in this country. They are made by coating finely shredded onions with a spicy batter.

SERVES 6-8

150g/6oz besan (gram or chick-pea flour)
1 tsp salt or to taste
Pinch of bicarbonate of soda
1 tbsp ground rice
2 tsps ground cumin
2 tsps ground coriander
½-1 tsp chilli powder
1-2 fresh green chillies, finely chopped and
   seeded if a milder flavour is preferred
2 large onions, sliced into half rings and
   separated
200ml/7fl oz water
Oil for deep frying

1. Sieve the besan and add the salt, bicarbonate of soda, ground rice, cumin, coriander, chilli powder and green chillies; mix well.

2. Now add the onions and mix thoroughly.

3. Gradually add the water and keep mixing until a soft but thick batter is formed and the onions are thoroughly coated with this batter.

4. Heat the oil over medium heat (*it is important to heat the oil to the correct temperature – 160-180° C*). To test this, take a tiny amount of the batter, about the size of a seed of a lemon and drop it in the oil. If it floats up to the surface immediately but without turning brown, the oil is at the correct temperature.

5. Using a tablespoon put in as many small amounts (about half a tablespoon) of the onion/batter mix as the pan will hold in a single layer. Take care not to make these amounts too large as this will result in the outside of the bhajiyas being overdone while the insides remain uncooked.

6. Reduce the heat to low as the bhajiyas need to be fried over a gentle heat to ensure that the batter at the centre of the bhajiyas is cooked, and stays soft, whilst the outside turns golden brown and crisp. This should take about 10-12 minutes for each batch.

7. Drain the bhajiyas on absorbent paper.

TIME Preparation takes 15-20 minutes, cooking takes 45-50 minutes.

SERVING IDEAS Serve on their own with drinks or with a selection of chutneys as a starter.
Suitable for freezing.

BARRAH KABAB (MARINATED LAMB CHOPS)

A wonderful dish which can be served as a starter or a main course.
The chops are marinated in a spice-laced yogurt mixture.
The yogurt tenderises the chops and also prepares the meat to absorb
the spices better.

SERVES 6-8

900g/2lbs lamb chump chops
½ tsp ground nutmeg
½ tsp ground black pepper
½ tsp ground cinnamon
½ tsp cayenne or chilli powder
½ tsp ground turmeric
2 cloves garlic, peeled
2 tbsps coarsely chopped onions
½-inch cube of root ginger, peeled and
 chopped
125g/5oz thick set natural yogurt
½ tsp salt or to taste
1 tbsp cooking oil
1 tsp ground cumin
1 tbsp sesame seeds

1. Trim off excess fat from the chops and flatten each chop with a meat mallet or a rolling pin. Wipe clean with a damp cloth.

2. Put all ingredients except chops, oil, cumin and sesame seeds, into an electric liquidiser or food processor and blend to a purée.

3. Put the chops into a large bowl and pour the blended ingredients over them.

4. Using your fingers, rub the marinade well into each chop.

5. Cover the container with cling film and leave to marinate for at least 8 hours in a cool place or overnight in the refrigerator.

6. Preheat oven to 219°C/425°F/Gas Mark 7.

7. Line a roasting tin with aluminium foil (this will help reflect heat and keep your roasting tin clean).

8. Arrange the chops on the roasting tin in a single layer (reserve any remaining marinade) and cook in the centre of the oven for 10 minutes – turning the chops over once. Reduce heat to 200°C/400°F/ Gas Mark 6.

9. Mix the remaining marinade with the oil and cumin. Brush the chops with this and sprinkle half the sesame seeds on top. Return the tray to the upper part of the oven for 10 minutes. Turn the chops over and brush this side with the remaining marinade mixture and sprinkle the rest of the sesame seeds as before. Cook for a further 10-15 minutes.

TIME Preparation takes 20-25 minutes plus 8 hours to marinate, cooking takes 30-35 minutes.

SERVING IDEAS Serve as a starter with plenty of raw onion rings, sprinkled with lemon juice, wedges of cucumber and crisp lettuce leaves; or as a main course with Plain Boiled Rice and Mixed Vegetable Curry.
Suitable for freezing.

CHICKEN OR TURKEY PAKORAS

These delicious pakoras can be made with cooked as well as raw meat and it is therefore an excellent and unusual way to use left over Christmas turkey or Sunday roast. Raw chicken breast has been used for the recipe below, as they remain more succulent than cooked meat.

SERVES 6-8

150ml/5fl oz water

1 medium-size onion, coarsely chopped

2-3 cloves garlic, peeled and coarsely chopped

1-2 fresh green chillies, coarsely chopped; remove the seeds if you prefer a mild flavour

2 tbsps chopped coriander leaves

125g/5oz besan or gram flour/chick pea flour, sieved

1 tsp ground coriander

1 tsp ground cumin

½ tsp garam masala

½ tsp chilli powder

1 tsp salt or to taste

Pinch of bicarbonate of soda

325g/12oz fresh, boneless and skinless chicken or turkey breast

Oil for deep frying

1. Put 90ml/3fl oz water from the specified amount into an electric liquidiser followed by the onion, garlic, green chillies and coriander leaves. Blend until smooth. Alternatively, process the ingredients in a food processor without the water.

2. In a large bowl, mix the besan, coriander, cumin, garam masala, chilli powder, salt and bicarbonate of soda.

3. Add the liquidised ingredients and mix thoroughly.

4. Add the remaining water and mix well to form a thick paste.

5. Cut the chicken into pieces and gently mix into the paste until the pieces are fully coated.

6. Heat the oil over medium heat; when hot, using a tablespoon, put in one piece of besan-coated chicken/turkey at a time until you have as many as the pan will hold in a single layer without overcrowding it. Make sure that each piece is fully coated with the paste.

7. Adjust heat to low and fry the pakoras for 10-15 minutes turning them over half way through. Remove the pakoras with a perforated spoon and drain on absorbent paper.

TIME Preparation takes 20 minutes, cooking takes 30 minutes.

BOTI KABAB

Tender boneless lamb is the traditional meat used for these kababs. They are marinated in a spice-laced yogurt dressing before cooking.

SERVES 6

700g/1½lbs boned leg of lamb
2 small cloves of garlic, peeled and
    chopped
2 tbsps chopped coriander leaves
2 tbsps lemon juice
75g/3oz thick set natural yogurt
Salt to taste
½ tsp ground turmeric
2 tbsps cooking oil

Grind the following 4 ingredients in a coffee grinder:
6 green cardamons (with the skin)
1 cinnamon stick, 1-inch long
2-3 dried red chillies
1 tbsp coriander seeds

To garnish
Thinly sliced onion rings, separated
Crisp lettuce leaves
Wedges of cucumber

---

1. Wash the meat and dry with a cloth.
2. Prick all over with a sharp knife and cut into 1½-inch cubes.

3. Put the garlic, coriander leaves, lemon juice and yogurt into a liquidiser or food processor and blend until smooth. Add the salt, turmeric and the ground ingredients.

4. Put the meat into a bowl and add the liquidised ingredients.

5. Mix thoroughly, cover and leave to marinate for 6-8 hours (or overnight in the refrigerator).

6. Preheat grill to high.

7. Line the grill pan with a piece of aluminium foil (this will reflect heat and also keep your grill pan clean).

8. Thread meat onto skewers leaving about ¼-inch gap between each piece.

9. Mix any remaining marinade with the oil and keep aside.

10. Place the skewers on the prepared grill pan and grill the kababs for 2-3 minutes.

11. Turn the skewers over and grill for a further 2-3 minutes.

12. Reduce heat to medium. Brush the kababs with the oil/marinade mixture and grill for 6-8 minutes.

13. Turn the skewers over and brush the kababs with the remaining oil/marinade mixture. Grill for a further 6-8 minutes.

TIME Preparation takes 20 minutes plus time needed for marinating, cooking takes 15-20 minutes.

SERVING IDEAS Serve as a starter, using ingredients given for garnishing. Serve on cocktail sticks with drinks or as a side dish for a dinner party.

VARIATION Use fillet of pork.

WATCHPOINT Do not overcook the Kababs: follow the cooking time precisely so that the Kababs remain succulent after cooking.

MUSHROOM BHAJI

Although mushrooms are not widely used in India, the Indian restaurants in this country have popularised the use of mushrooms in Indian cookery. Mushroom Bhaji appears to be one of the most popular of them all.

SERVES 4

3-4 tbsps cooking oil
1 medium-sized onion, finely chopped
2-3 cloves garlic, peeled and crushed
½ tsp ground turmeric
½ tsp chilli powder
1 tsp ground coriander
1 tsp ground cumin
¾ tsp salt or to taste
1 tbsp tomato purée
225g/8oz mushrooms, chopped

1. Heat the oil over medium heat and fry the onions until they are lightly browned.

2. Lower heat and add the garlic, turmeric, chilli powder, coriander and cumin. Stir and fry the spices and add about 1 tbsp water to prevent the spices from sticking to the bottom of the pan. As soon as this water dries up, add a little more. Continue doing this until you have fried the spices for about 5 minutes.

3. Add the salt and tomato purée, mix well and add the mushrooms. Stir until the ingredients are thoroughly mixed.

4. Sprinkle about 2 tbsps water and cover the pan. Simmer for 10 minutes.

5. The finished dish should have a little amount of gravy, but it should not be runny. If it appears to be a little runny, take the lid off and let the liquid evaporate until the gravy is reasonably thick.

TIME Preparation takes 15 minutes, cooking takes 20 minutes.

CHICKEN TIKKA

*Chicken Tikka is one of the most popular chicken dishes cooked in the Tandoor,
the Indian clay oven. This recipe is adapted to cook the chicken in the
conventional oven at a high temperature.*

SERVES 4

450g/1lb boneless, skinned chicken breast
1 tsp salt
Juice of ½ a lemon
½ tsp tandoori colour or a few drops of
    red food colouring mixed with
    1 tbsp tomato purée
2 cloves garlic, peeled and coarsely
    chopped
½-inch cube of root ginger, peeled and
    coarsely chopped
2 tsps ground coriander
½ tsp ground allspice or garam masala
¼ of a whole nutmeg, finely grated
½ tsp ground turmeric
125g/5oz thick set natural yogurt
4 tbsps corn or vegetable oil
½ tsp chilli powder

1. Cut the chicken into 1-inch cubes. Sprinkle with ½ tsp salt from the specified amount, and the lemon juice – mix thoroughly, cover and keep aside for 30 minutes.

2. Put the rest of the ingredients into an electric food processor or liquidiser and blend until smooth.

3. Put this marinade into a sieve and hold the sieve over the chicken pieces. Press the marinade through the sieve with the back of a metal spoon until only a very coarse mixture is left.

4. Coat the chicken thoroughly with the sieved marinade, cover the container and leave to marinate for 6-8 hours or overnight in the refrigerator.

5. Preheat the oven to 230°C/450°F/Gas Mark 8.

6. Line a roasting tin with aluminium foil (this will help to maintain the high level of temperature required to cook the chicken quickly without drying it out).

7. Thread the chicken onto skewers, leaving ¼-inch gap between each piece (this is necessary for the heat to reach all sides of the chicken).

8. Place the skewers in the prepared roasting tin and brush with some of the remaining marinade.

9. Cook in the centre of the oven for 6-8 minutes.

10. Take the tin out of the oven, turn the skewers over and brush the pieces of chicken with the remaining marinade.

11. Return the tin to the oven and cook for a further 6-8 minutes.

12. Shake off any excess liquid from the chicken. (Strain the excess liquid and keep aside for Chicken Tikka Masala)

13. Place the skewers on a serving dish. You may take the tikka off the skewers if you wish, but allow the meat to cool slightly before removing from the skewers.

TIME Preparation takes 30-35 minutes plus time needed to marinate,
cooking takes 15-18 minutes.

MEAT SAMOSAS

*The ever-popular Samosas make a wonderful treat on any occasion. In India,
they are a familiar sight at wedding receptions and cocktail parties.*

MAKES 18 Samosas

2 tbsps cooking oil
2 medium-sized onions, finely chopped
225g/8oz lean mince, lamb or beef
3-4 cloves garlic, peeled and crushed
½-inch cube of root ginger, finely grated
½ tsp ground turmeric
2 tsps ground coriander
1½ tsps ground cumin
½-1 tsp chilli powder
½ tsp salt or to taste
125ml/4fl oz warm water
150g/6oz frozen garden peas
2 tbsps desiccated coconut
1 tsp garam masala
1-2 fresh green chillies, finely chopped and
   seeded if a milder flavour is preferred
2 tbsps chopped coriander leaves
1 tbsp lemon juice

1. Heat the oil over medium heat and fry the onions until they are lightly browned.

2. Add the mince, garlic and ginger. Stir and fry until all the liquid evaporates and adjust heat to low.

3. Add the turmeric, coriander, cumin, chilli powder and salt. Stir and fry until mince is lightly browned.

4. Add the water and the peas, bring to the boil, cover and simmer for 25–30 minutes. If there is any liquid left, take the lid off and cook the mince over medium heat until it is completely dry, stirring frequently.

5. Stir in the coconut, garam masala, green chillies and coriander leaves.

6. Remove from heat and add the lemon juice. Cool thoroughly before filling the Samosas.

For the pastry

225g/8oz plain flour
50g/2oz ghee or butter
½ tsp salt
75 ml/2½ fl oz warm water
Oil for deep frying

1. Add the butter and salt to the flour. Rub in well.

2. Mix a soft dough by adding the water. Knead until the dough feels soft and velvety to the touch.

3. Divide the dough into 9 balls. Rotate each ball between your palms in a circular motion, then press it down to make a flat cake.

4. Roll out each flat cake into 4-inch discs

and cut into two. Use each semicircle of pastry as one envelope.

5. Moisten the straight edge with a little warm water.

6. Fold the semicircle of pastry in half to form a triangular cone.

7. Join the straight edges by pressing them hard into each other. Make sure that there are no gaps.

8. Fill these cones with the filling, leaving about ¼-inch border on the top of the cone.

9. Now moisten the top edges and press them hard together.

10. Deep fry the samosas over gentle heat until they are golden brown and drain on absorbent paper.

SPICED POTATO BITES

In Indian cookery, potatoes are used very imaginatively. Here, boiled potatoes are cut into small pieces and sautéed until they are brown and then flavoured with a light sprinkling of spices.

SERVES 6-8

700g/1½lbs potatoes
4 tbsps cooking oil
½ tbsp salt or to taste
¼ tsp garam masala
½ tsp ground cumin
½ tsp ground coriander
¼ - ½ tsp chilli powder

1. Boil the potatoes in their jacket, cool thoroughly, peel and dice them into 1-inch cubes.

2. In a wide shallow pan, preferably non-stick or cast iron, heat the oil over medium heat. It is important to have the right pan otherwise the potatoes will stick.

3. Add the potatoes and spread them evenly around the pan. Brown the potatoes evenly, stirring them occasionally.

4. When the potatoes are brown, sprinkle over the salt, garam masala, cumin, coriander and the chilli powder. Stir gently and mix until the potatoes are fully coated with the spices. Remove from the heat.

TIME Preparation takes 30 minutes to boil the potatoes plus time to cool them, cooking takes 10-12 minutes.

SERVING IDEAS Serve on cocktail sticks with drinks.

WATCHPOINT The potatoes must be allowed to cool thoroughly. Hot or warm potatoes crumble easily and therefore cannot be cut into neat pieces.

Chapter 2
Main Meals

Fish and Seafood

FISH SHAHJAHANI

*A rich, but easy to prepare fish dish which is named after the Mughal Emperor
Shahjahan, who was noted for his love of good food.*

SERVES 4

700g/1½lbs fillet of any white fish
75g/3oz roasted cashews
125ml/4fl oz single cream
50g/2oz unsalted butter
225g/8oz onions, finely sliced
2-inch piece of cinnamon stick, broken up
4 green cardamoms, split open the top of
    each pod
2 whole cloves
1-2 fresh green chillies, sliced lengthwise;
    seeded if a milder flavour is preferred
1 tsp ground turmeric
175ml/6fl oz warm water
1 tsp salt or to taste
1 tbsp lemon juice

1. Rinse the fish gently in cold water, dry on absorbent paper and cut into 2.5 × 5cm/1 × 2-inch pieces.

2. Put the cashews and the cream in an electric blender and blend to a reasonably fine mixture.

3. In a wide, shallow pan melt the butter over medium heat and fry onions, cinnamon, cardamom, cloves and green chillies until the onions are lightly browned (6-8 minutes). Stir in the turmeric.

4. Add the water and salt and arrange the fish in a single layer. Bring to the boil, cover the pan and simmer for 2-3 minutes.

5. Now add the cashew/cream mixture and stir gently until the pieces of fish are well coated. Cover the pan again and simmer for a further 2-3 minutes.

6. Remove from heat and gently stir in the lemon juice.

TIME Preparation takes 15 minutes, cooking takes 15-20 minutes.

VARIATION Use potatoes which have been boiled in their jackets, peeled and diced

WATCHPOINT It is important to use a wide shallow pan so that the fish can be arranged in a single layer to prevent them from breaking up during cooking.

Fish and Seafood

TANDOORI FISH

A firm-fleshed white fish is ideal for this dish; it is not necessary to use an expensive fish. The fish should be handled carefully as most white fish tend to flake during cooking.

SERVES 4

450g/1lb fillet or steak of any white fish

2 cloves garlic, peeled and coarsely
    chopped

¼-inch cube of root ginger, peeled and
    coarsely chopped

½ tsp salt

1 tsp ground cumin

1 tsp ground coriander

½ tsp garam masala

¼-½ tsp chilli powder

¼ tsp Tandoori colour or a few drops of red
    food colouring mixed with 1 tbsp tomato
    purée

Juice of half a lemon

3 tbsps water

2 tbsps cooking oil

*Mix the following ingredients
in a small bowl*

2 heaped tbsps flour

½ tsp chilli powder

¼ tsp salt

1. Wash the fish and dry on absorbent paper. Cut into 1-inch squares. If using frozen fish, defrost it thoroughly and dry on absorbent paper before cutting it.

2. Add the salt to the ginger and garlic and crush to a smooth pulp.

3. In a small bowl, mix together the ginger/garlic pulp, cumin, coriander, garam masala, chilli powder and Tandoori colour or tomato purée mix. Add the lemon juice and water and mix thoroughly. Keep aside.

4. Heat the oil over medium heat in a non-stick or cast iron frying pan. Dust each piece of fish in the seasoned flour and put in the hot oil in a single layer, leave plenty of room in the pan. Fry for 5 minutes, 2½ minutes each side, and drain on absorbent paper. Now return all the fish to the pan.

5. Hold a sieve over the pan and pour the liquid spice mixture into it. Press with the back of a metal spoon until the mixture in the sieve looks dry and very coarse; discard this mixture.

6. Stir gently and cook over medium heat until the fish is fully coated with the spices and the liquid dries up. Remove from heat.

TIME Preparation takes 15 minutes, cooking takes 15-20 minutes.

SERVING IDEAS Serve garnished with shredded lettuce leaves, sliced
cucumber and raw onion rings.
Suitable for freezing.

Fish and Seafood

MASALA MACHCHI

Masala Machchi or spicy fish is made by marinating fish in lemon juice and spices. The lemon juice gives the fish a rather smooth and velvety texture.

SERVES 4

Juice of half a lemon

1 small onion, peeled and coarsely chopped

2-3 cloves garlic, peeled and coarsely chopped

1-inch cube of root ginger, peeled and coarsely chopped

1-2 fresh green chillies, chopped; seed the chillies if you like a milder flavour

3 tbsps chopped coriander leaves

1 tsp salt or to taste

450g/1lb fillet of any white fish

90ml/3fl oz oil for shallow frying

To coat the fish

3 tbsps plain flour

1 egg, beaten

¼ tsp salt

¼ tsp chilli powder

1. Put the lemon juice, onion, garlic, ginger, green chillies, coriander leaves and 1 tsp salt into an electric liquidiser and blend until smooth.

2. Wash the fish gently and pat dry with absorbent paper. If you are using frozen fish, defrost thoroughly and then dry as for fresh fish.

3. Cut the fish into 1½ × 1-inch pieces. Put a light coating of the spice paste on all sides of each piece of fish, cover the container and leave to marinate in a cool place for 2-3 hours, or overnight in the refrigerator.

4. Mix the flour with the salt and chilli powder. Dust each piece of fish lightly with this, then dip in the beaten egg. Shallow fry in a single layer over medium heat until brown on both sides (2-3 minutes on each side). Drain on absorbent paper. Alternatively, deep fry the fish until golden brown and drain on absorbent paper.

TIME Preparation takes 15-20 minutes, cooking takes 12-15 minutes.

Fish and Seafood

SPICED SARDINES

Fresh sardines are easily available from early summer to late autumn. The preparation below is simple and tastes excellent.

SERVES 4

8 fresh sardines (about 700g/1½lb)

1 tsp salt or to taste

3-4 cloves garlic, peeled and coarsely chopped

The juice of half a lemon

½ tsp ground turmeric

½-1 tsp chilli powder

3 heaped tbsps plain flour

60ml/2½fl oz cooking oil

1. Scale and clean the fish. Wash gently in cold water and dry on absorbent paper.

2. Add the salt to the garlic and crush to a smooth pulp.

3. Mix all the ingredients together, except the fish, flour and oil, in a small bowl.

4. Put the fish in a wide shallow dish and pour the marinade over. Spread it gently on both sides of the fish, cover and refrigerate for 2-4 hours.

5. Heat the oil over medium heat. Dip each fish in the flour and coat it thoroughly. Fry until golden brown on both sides (2-3 minutes each side). Drain on absorbent paper.

TIME Preparation takes 20 minutes plus 2-4 hours to marinate, cooking takes 6-8 minutes

Fish and Seafood

BENGAL FISH CURRY

The abundance of fish in the Bay of Bengal has enabled the people of this north eastern part of India to develop many delicious dishes using fish. In the recipe below, the fish is cooked entirely in natural yogurt which, with the addition of a little gram flour, gives it an unusual touch.

SERVES 4

700g/1½lbs firm fleshed fish such as river trout, grey or red mullet
1 tsp ground turmeric
1¼ tsps salt or to taste
5 tbsps cooking oil
1 large onion, finely chopped
¼-in cube of root ginger – peeled and finely chopped or grated
1 tbsp ground coriander
½-1 tsp chilli powder
1 tsp paprika
275g/10oz thick set natural yogurt
4-6 whole fresh green chillies
1-2 cloves of garlic, peeled and crushed
1 tbsp besan (gram or chick pea flour)
2 tbsps chopped coriander leaves (optional)

1. Clean and wash the fish and pat dry.

2. Cut each fish in to 1½-inch pieces.

3. Gently rub into the fish ¼ tsp turmeric and ¼ tsp salt from the specified amount and put it aside for 15-20 minutes.

4. Meanwhile, heat the oil over medium heat; use a pan wide enough to hold the fish in a single layer and fry onion and ginger until the onions are lightly browned (6-7 minutes), stirring frequently.

5. Add coriander, remaining turmeric, chilli powder and the paprika – adjust heat to low and fry for 1-2 minutes, stirring continuously.

6. Beat the yogurt with a fork until smooth and add to the onion and spice mixture, adjust heat to medium, add the whole green chillies, the remaining salt and the garlic. Stir and mix well.

7. Arrange the pieces of fish in this liquid in a single layer and bring to the boil. Cover and cook over low heat for 5-6 minutes.

8. Blend the besan with a little water to make a pouring consistency. Strain this over the fish curry, stir gently, and mix. Cover and cook for 2-3 minutes.

9. Remove from heat and gently mix in half the coriander leaves.

10. Transfer the fish curry into a serving dish and garnish with the remaining coriander leaves (if used).

TIME Preparation takes 20-25 minutes, cooking takes 20 minutes.

Fish and Seafood

PRAWN CHILLI MASALA

*This is a delicate but richly flavoured dish. In India, only fresh and juicy king
prawns will do, but standard peeled prawns can be used for this recipe.*

SERVES 4

75g/3oz unsalted butter
6 green cardamoms, split open the top of
    each pod
1-inch cube of root ginger, peeled and
    finely grated
3-4 cloves garlic, peeled and crushed
1 tbsp ground coriander
½ tsp ground turmeric
450g/1lb fresh peeled prawns
125g/5oz thick set natural yogurt
90ml/3fl oz water
1 tsp sugar
1 tsp salt or to taste
25g/1oz ground almonds
4-6 whole fresh green chillies
100g/4oz finely chopped onions
2 fresh green chillies, seeded and minced
½ tsp garam masala
1 tbsp chopped coriander leaves

1. Melt 50g/2oz butter from the specified amount over gentle heat and add the whole cardamoms, fry for 30 seconds and add the ginger and garlic. Stir and cook for 1 minute, then add the ground coriander and turmeric. Stir and fry for 30 seconds.

2. Add the prawns, turn the heat up to medium and cook for 5-6 minutes, stirring frequently.

3. Beat the yogurt until smooth, gradually add the water and beat until well blended. Add this mixture to the prawns, stir in the sugar and the salt, cover the pan and simmer for 5-6 minutes.

4. Add the ground almonds and the whole green chillies and cook, uncovered, for 5 minutes.

5. Meanwhile, fry the onions in the remaining 25g/1oz butter until they are just soft, but not brown. Add the minced green chillies and the garam masala; stir and fry for a further 1-2 minutes. Stir this mixture into the prawns along with any butter left in the pan. Remove the pan from the heat.

6. Put the prawns in a serving dish and garnish with the coriander leaves.

TIME Preparation takes 15 minutes, cooking takes 20-25 minutes.

Classic Chicken Dishes

MAKKHANI MURGHI

Makkhani Murghi, or Chicken in a Butter Sauce, is rich, delicious and irresistible! It is bound to be an overwhelming success with your dinner guests!

SERVES 6-8

1kg/2.2lbs chicken breast, skinned

1¼ tsps salt or to taste

1-inch cube of root ginger, peeled and coarsely chopped

4-6 cloves garlic, peeled and coarsely chopped

125g/5oz thick set natural yogurt

The juice of 1 lemon

Grind the following 5 ingredients in a coffee grinder

1 cinnamon stick, 2-inches long; broken up

8 green cardamoms with the skin

6 whole cloves

8-10 red chillies

6-8 white peppercorns

2 tbsps cooking oil

2 tbsps tomato purée

225g/8oz butter

400g/14oz can of tomatoes

2 cinnamon sticks, each 2-inches long; broken up

150ml/5fl oz single cream

1. Wash and dry the chicken and cut into 4 × 2-inch strips.

2. Add the salt to the ginger and garlic and crush to a smooth pulp.

3. Combine the yogurt, lemon juice and the ground spices and beat until the mixture is smooth. Marinate the chicken in this mixture, cover the container and leave it in a cool place for 2-4 hours or overnight in the refrigerator.

4. Heat the oil over medium heat and add the ginger/garlic pulp, stir and fry for 1 minute. Add the chicken and stir and fry for 10 minutes.

5. Add the tomato purée and butter, cook on low heat, uncovered, for 10 minutes. Remove the pan from the heat, cover and keep aside.

6. Put the tomatoes and the cinnamon sticks in a separate pan, bring to the boil, cover and simmer for 10 minutes. Remove the lid and adjust heat to medium; cook uncovered until the liquid is reduced to half its original volume (6-8 minutes). Remove the pan from the heat and allow the tomato mixture to cool slightly.

7. Sieve the cooked tomatoes, discard the cinnamon sticks. Add the sieved tomatoes to the chicken and place the pan over medium heat. Bring the liquid to the boil, reduce heat to low and cook, uncovered, for 5-6 minutes.

8. Add the cream, stir and mix well, and simmer uncovered for about 5 minutes. Remove from the heat.

TIME Preparation takes 20-25 minutes plus time needed for marinating, cooking takes 40-45 minutes.

Classic Chicken Dishes

CORIANDER CHICKEN

Coriander Chicken is quick and easy to make, it tastes wonderful and looks very impressive – a perfect choice for any dinner party menu.

SERVES 4-6

1kg/2.2lbs chicken joints, skinned
2-4 cloves garlic, peeled and crushed
125g/5oz thick set natural yogurt
5 tbsps cooking oil
1 large onion, finely sliced
2 tbsps ground coriander
½ tsp ground black pepper
1 tsp ground mixed spice
½ tsp ground turmeric
½ tsp cayenne pepper or chilli powder
125ml/4fl oz warm water
1 tsp salt or to taste
25g/1oz ground almonds
2 hard-boiled eggs, sliced
¼ tsp paprika

1. Cut each chicken joint into two, mix thoroughly with the crushed garlic and the yogurt. Cover the container and leave to marinate in a cool place for 2-4 hours or overnight in the refrigerator.

2. Heat the oil over medium heat and fry the onions until they are golden brown (6-8 minutes). Remove with a slotted spoon and keep aside.

3. In the same oil, fry the coriander, ground pepper, ground mixed spice and turmeric for 15 seconds and add the chicken along with all the marinade in the container.

4. Adjust heat to medium-high and fry the chicken until it changes colour (5-6 minutes).

5. Adjust the cayenne or chilli powder, water, salt, and the fried onion slices. Bring to the boil, cover the pan and simmer until the chicken is tender (about 30 minutes).

6. Stir in the ground almonds and remove from heat.

TIME Preparation takes 20 minutes plus time needed for marinating, cooking takes 45-50 minutes.

WATCHPOINT Reduce cooking time if boneless chicken is used.

Classic Chicken Dishes

MURGHI NAWABI

*This is a classic example of the popular Mughal cuisine which is noted for its
delicate flavourings and rich smooth sauces. The chicken is marinated in yogurt
and turmeric and simmered in delicately flavoured coconut milk.*

SERVES 4-6

1kg/2.2lbs chicken joints, skinned

125g/5oz thick set natural yogurt

½ tsp ground turmeric

3-4 cloves garlic, peeled and coarsely
chopped

1-inch cube of root ginger, peeled and
coarsely chopped

4-6 dried red chillies

50g/2oz ghee or unsalted butter

2 large onions, finely sliced

1 tsp caraway seeds

1 tsp garam masala

1¼ tsps salt or to taste

225ml/8fl oz warm water plus 90ml/3fl oz
cold water

85g/3½oz creamed coconut, cut into small
pieces

75g/3oz raw cashews

2 hard-boiled eggs, sliced

¼ tsp paprika

---

1. Cut each chicken joint into two pieces
(separate leg from thigh and cut each breast
into two pieces). Wash the chicken and dry
on absorbent paper.

2. Beat the yogurt and turmeric powder
together until smooth. Add to the chicken
and mix thoroughly, cover the container
and leave to marinate for 4-6 hours or
overnight in the refrigerator.

3. Put the garlic, ginger and red chillies in
an electric liquidiser and add just enough
water to facilitate blade movement and
mixing. Blend until the ingredients are
smooth. Alternatively, crush the garlic,
ginger and finely chop the chillies.

4. Melt the ghee or butter over medium
heat and fry the onions until they are brown
(8-10 minutes). Remove the pan from heat
and, using a wooden spatula, press the
onions to the side of the pan in order to
squeeze out excess fat. Transfer the onions
onto a plate and keep aside.

5. Place the pan back on heat and fry the
caraway seeds and garam masala for 30
seconds. Add the blended ingredients. Stir
briskly and add the chicken, fried onions
and salt. Fry the chicken for 5-6 minutes,
stirring frequently and lowering heat as the
chicken is heated through. If there is any
yogurt marinade left in the container add
this to the chicken.

6. Add the water and the creamed coconut.
Bring to the boil, cover the pan and simmer
until the chicken is tender and the gravy is
thick (30-35 minutes). Stir occasionally
during this time.

7. Meanwhile, put the cashews into an
electric blender and add the cold water and
blend until smooth. Add the cashew paste
to the chicken during the last 5 minutes of
cooking time. Simmer uncovered for 4-5
minutes, stirring frequently.

8. Put the chicken into a serving dish and
garnish with the sliced eggs. Sprinkle the
paprika on top.

Classic Chicken Dishes

CHICKEN LIVER MASALA

*Curried liver is quite a popular item in India, particularly with Muslims.
This recipe is made more interesting by adding diced potatoes and
frozen garden peas.*

SERVES 4

450g/1lb chicken liver
4 tbsps cooking oil
1 large onion finely chopped
1 cinnamon stick, 2-inches long, broken up
225g/8oz potatoes, peeled and diced
1¼ tsps salt or to taste
90ml/3fl oz warm water
3-4 cloves garlic, peeled and crushed

*Make a paste of the following 4 ingredients
by adding 2 tsps water*
2 tsps ground coriander
1 tsp ground cumin
1 tsp ground turmeric
½ tsp chilli powder

1 small tin of tomatoes
100g/4oz frozen garden peas
2-3 fresh green chillies, whole
½ tsp garam masala

---

1. Clean the liver, remove all skin and
gristle and cut roughly into ½-inch pieces.

2. Heat 2 tbsps oil over medium heat and
fry the onions and cinnamon stick until the
onions are soft.

3. Add the potatoes and ¼ tsp salt and stir

fry the potatoes for about 2 minutes.

4. Add the water, cover the pan and simmer
until the potatoes are tender.

5. Meanwhile, heat the remaining oil over
medium heat in a heavy-based, wide pan. A
nonstick or cast iron pan is ideal as the liver
needs to be stir-fried over high heat.

6. Add the garlic and stir fry for 30 seconds.

7. Add the spice paste, reduce heat to low,
and stir and fry for about 2 minutes.

8. Add half the tomatoes, along with some
of the juice, stir and cook for a further 2-3
minutes, breaking the tomatoes with the
spoon.

9. When the mixture is fairly dry, add the
liver and adjust heat to medium-high. Stir-
fry the liver for 3-4 minutes.

10. Add the remaining tomatoes and the
juice, stir and fry for 5-6 minutes.

11. Cover the pan and simmer for 6-8
minutes.

12. Add the potatoes, peas, green chillies
and the remaining salt and cook for 1-2
minutes. Adjust heat to medium and cook,
uncovered, for a further 4-5 minutes.

13. Stir in the garam masala and remove
from heat.

TIME Preparation takes 20-25 minutes, cooking takes 36-40 minutes.

TANDOORI CHICKEN

The Tandoor, because of its fierce but even distribution of heat, enables meat to cook quickly, forming a light crust on the outside but leaving the inside moist and succulent.
It is possible to achieve perfectly satisfactory results by using a conventional gas or electric oven at the highest temperature setting, though the distinctive flavour of clay-cooked chicken will not be achieved.

SERVES 4-6

1.2kg/2½lbs chicken joints, legs or breast or a combination of the two
1 tsp salt or to taste
Juice of half a lemon
½-inch cube of root ginger, peeled and coarsely chopped
2-3 small cloves of garlic, peeled and coarsely chopped
1 fresh green chilli, coarsely chopped and seeded if a milder flavour is required
2 tbsps chopped coriander leaves
75g/3oz thick set natural yogurt
1 tsp ground coriander
½ tsp ground cumin
1 tsp garam masala
¼ tsp freshly ground black pepper
½ tsp Tandoori colour (available from Indian grocers in powder form), or a few drops of red food colouring mixed with 1 tbsp tomato purée

1. Remove skin from the chicken and cut each piece into two. With a sharp knife, make 2-3 slits in each piece. Rub salt and lemon juice into the chicken pieces and set aside for half an hour.

2. Meanwhile, put the ginger, garlic, green chillies, coriander leaves and the yogurt into a liquidiser and blend until smooth. Add the rest of the ingredients and blend again.

3. Pour and spread the marinade all over the chicken, especially into the slits. Cover the container with cling film and leave to marinate for 6-8 hours or overnight in the refrigerator.

4. Preheat oven to 240°C/475°F/Gas Mark 9. Line a roasting tin with aluminium foil (this will help to maintain the high level of heat required to cook the chicken) and arrange the chicken pieces in it. Place the roasting tin in the centre of the oven and bake for 25-30 minutes, turning the pieces over carefully as they brown and basting with juice in the roasting tin as well as any remaining marinade.

5. Remove from the oven, lift each piece with a pair of tongs and shake off any excess liquid.

TIME Preparation takes 20-25 minutes, cooking takes 25-30 minutes.

Classic Chicken Dishes

MURGHI JHAL FREZI

This delicious and relatively easy dish to cook, with thick spice paste clinging to the pieces of chicken, makes it an irresistible choice for entertaining.

SERVES 4-6

1kg/2.2lbs chicken joints

3 large onions, finely chopped

175ml/6fl oz water

1-inch cube of root ginger, peeled and grated

2-4 cloves garlic, peeled and crushed

1 tsp ground coriander

1 tsp ground cumin

1 tsp ground ajwain or caraway

½ tsp ground turmeric

½ chilli powder

2 cinnamon sticks, 2-inch long each, broken up

2 black cardamoms, split open the top of each pod

4 whole cloves

5 tbsps cooking oil

1¼ tsp salt or to taste

1 tbsp tomato purée

1-2 fresh green chillies, sliced lengthwise; seeded for a milder flavour

2 tbsps chopped coriander leaves

1. Skin and cut each joint into two, separate leg from thigh and cut each breast into two pieces, wash and dry on absorbent paper.

2. Put the chicken in a saucepan, add half the chopped onions, water, ginger, garlic, coriander, cumin, ajwain, turmeric, chilli powder, cinnamon, cardamom and cloves. Bring to the boil, stir and mix thoroughly. Cover and simmer for 20-25 minutes.

3. In a separate pan, heat the oil over medium heat and fry the rest of the onions until they are golden brown.

4. Remove each piece of chicken with a pair of tongs and add to the onions. Fry over medium heat until the chicken is brown (about 5 minutes).

5. Now add half the spiced liquid in which the chicken was cooked, stir and fry for 4-5 minutes. Add the rest of the liquid and fry for a further 4-5 minutes.

6. Add salt, tomato purée, green chillies and coriander leaves, stir and fry on low heat for 5-6 minutes. Remove from heat.

TIME Preparation takes 20-25 minutes, cooking takes 45-50 minutes.

VARIATION Use lean pork instead of chicken.

WATCHPOINT Reduce the cooking time for boneless chicken and in stage 5, fry the chicken for a little longer to reach the paste-like consistency required.

Classic Chicken Dishes

CHICKEN CHAAT

Recipes do not have to be elaborate to be tasty, and Chicken Chaat is a perfect example. Cubes of chicken meat, stir-fried with a light coating of spices look impressive with a colourful salad and taste superb.

SERVES 4

700g/1½lbs chicken breast, skinned and boned

1 tsp salt or to taste

2-3 cloves garlic, peeled and coarsely chopped

2 tbsps cooking oil

1½ tsps ground coriander

¼ tsp ground turmeric

¼-½ tsp chilli powder

1½ tbsps lemon juice

2 tbsps finely chopped coriander leaves

1. Wash the chicken and dry on absorbent paper. Cut into 1-inch cubes.

2. Add the salt to the garlic and crush to a smooth pulp.

3. Heat the oil in a frying pan, preferably non-stick or cast iron, over medium heat.

4. Add the garlic and fry until it is lightly browned.

5. Add the chicken and fry for 6-7 minutes, stirring constantly.

6. Add the ground coriander, turmeric and chilli powder. Fry for 3-4 minutes, stirring frequently. Remove from heat and stir in the lemon juice and coriander leaves.

TIME Preparation takes 15 minutes, cooking takes 12-15 minutes.

Classic Chicken Dishes

CHICKEN KOHLAPURI

This delicious chicken dish comes from Kohlapur in southern India. The original recipe has a large amount of chillies as people in this part of India prefer a very hot flavour. For this recipe, however, the quantity of chillies has been reduced.

SERVES 4-6

1.4kg/2½lbs chicken joints, skinned
1 large onion, coarsely chopped
3-4 cloves garlic, peeled and coarsely chopped
1-inch cube of root ginger, peeled and coarsely chopped
6 tbsps cooking oil
1 tsp ground turmeric
2 tsps ground coriander
1½ tsps ground cumin
1-1¼ tsps chilli powder
1 small tin of tomatoes
1¼ tsps salt or to taste
180ml/6fl oz water
4-6 whole green chillies
1 tsp garam masala
2 tbsps chopped coriander leaves

1. Cut each chicken joint in two (separate legs from thighs or cut breast into 2-3 pieces); wash and dry on absorbent paper.

2. Place the onion, garlic and ginger in an electric food processor or liquidiser and blend to a smooth purée. You may need to add a little water if you are using a liquidiser.

3. Heat the oil over medium heat and add the liquidised ingredients. Stir and fry for 5-6 minutes.

4. Add turmeric, ground coriander, cumin and chilli powder; adjust heat to low and fry for 4-5 minutes stirring frequently.

5. Add half the tomatoes, stir and cook for 2-3 minutes.

6. Now add the chicken, stir and cook until chicken changes colour (4-5 minutes) and add the rest of the tomatoes, along with all the juice.

7. Add salt and water, bring to the boil, cover and simmer until the chicken is tender. Stir occasionally to ensure that the thickened gravy does not stick to the bottom of the pan.

8. Add the whole green chillies and garam masala, cover and simmer for 5 minutes.

9. Remove the pan from heat and stir in the coriander leaves.

TIME Preparation takes 15-20 minutes, cooking takes 55 minutes.

SERVING IDEAS Serve with Plain Boiled Rice and Mixed Vegetable Bhaji. Suitable for freezing.

WATCHPOINT In stage 3, it is important to fry the ingredients for the specified time so that the raw smell of the onions, ginger and garlic can be eliminated before adding the rest of the ingredients.

Classic Chicken Dishes

CHICKEN TIKKA MASALA

The delicate flavour of chicken smothered in almond and cream sauce makes this a wonderful choice for a dinner party or a special occasion menu.

SERVES 4

450g/1lb Chicken Tikka (see separate recipe)

½-inch cube of root ginger, peeled and coarsely chopped

2 cloves garlic, peeled and coarsely chopped

1 tsp salt or to taste

50g/2oz unsalted butter

1 small onion, finely chopped

¼ tsp ground turmeric

½ tsp ground cumin

½ tsp ground coriander

½ tsp garam masala

¼-½ tsp chilli powder

125ml/4fl oz liquid, made up of the reserved juice from the precooked Chicken Tikka and warm water

300ml/10fl oz double cream

2 heaped tbsps ground almonds

1. Mix together the ginger, garlic and ½ tsp salt from the specified amount and crush to a pulp. Keep the remaining salt aside for later use.

2. Melt the butter gently and fry the onions for 2-3 minutes.

3. Add the ginger/garlic paste and cook for 1 minute.

4. Stir in the turmeric and then the cumin, coriander, garam masala and chilli powder. Stir and cook for 2 minutes.

5. Add the liquid and stir gently.

6. Gradually add the cream and stir.

7. Add the remaining salt and simmer for 5 minutes and then add the chicken. Adjust heat to low, cover and cook for 10 minutes.

8. Stir in the ground almonds and simmer for 5-6 minutes.

9. Remove from heat.

TIME Preparation takes 10 minutes plus time needed to marinate the tikka, cooking takes 25 minutes plus time needed to cook the tikka.

Classic Chicken Dishes

CHICKEN KORMA

Korma is a classic north Indian dish and there are many variations, some of which are quite elaborate. The recipe below, though simple and prepared with readily available ingredients, has all the characteristic features of this classic dish.

SERVES 4-6

1.4kg/2½lbs chicken joints, skin removed

1-inch cube of root ginger, finely grated

125g/5oz thick set natural yogurt

1 small onion, coarsely chopped

3-4 dried red chillies

2-4 cloves garlic, peeled and coarsely
    chopped

5 tbsps cooking oil plus 2 tbsps extra oil

450g/1lb onions, finely sliced

1 tbsp ground coriander

½ tsp powdered black pepper

1 tsp garam masala

1 tsp ground turmeric

225ml/8fl oz warm water (reduce quantity if
    using boneless chicken)

75g/3oz creamed coconut, cut into small
    pieces

1¼ tsps salt or to taste

2 heaped tbsps ground almonds

Juice of ½ a lemon

---

1. Cut each chicken joint into half, separating leg from thigh and cutting each breast into two.

2. Mix with ginger and yogurt, cover and leave to marinate in a cool place for 2-4 hours or in the refrigerator overnight.

3. Place the chopped onion, red chillies and garlic in a liquidiser or food processor and liquidise to a smooth paste. You may need to add a little water if you are using a liquidiser.

4. Heat the 5 tbsps oil over medium heat and fry the sliced onions till they are golden brown. Remove the pan from the heat and using a slotted spoon, transfer the onions to another dish, Leave any remaining oil in the pan.

5. Place the pan in which the onions have been fried, over medium heat and add the other 2 tbsps cooking oil.

6. When hot, add the ground coriander, powdered pepper, garam masala and turmeric, stir rapidly (take the pan off the heat if the oil is too hot) and add the chicken along with the marinade. Adjust the heat to medium-high and fry the chicken for about 10 minutes, stirring frequently.

7. Add the liquidised spices and continue to fry for 6-8 minutes on low heat.

8. Add the water and the coconut and bring to the boil. Stir until coconut is dissolved. Add fried onion slices and salt.

9. Reduce heat to low, cover the pan and simmer until the chicken is tender (25-30 minutes). Sprinkle the ground almonds and mix well. Remove from heat and add the lemon juice.

TIME Preparation takes 15 minutes plus time needed to marinate, cooking takes 55 minutes.

Classic Chicken Dishes

CHICKEN DO-PIAZA

A fairly easy dish to prepare in which more than the usual quantity of onions are used. The name itself suggests the quantity of onions required, Do means twice and Piaz means onion. The literal translation would, therefore, be 'chicken with twice the amount of onions'

SERVES 4-6

1.4kg/2½lbs chicken joints, skin removed

1 large onion, coarsely chopped

1-inch cube of root ginger, peeled and
   coarsely chopped

3-4 cloves garlic, peeled and coarsely
   chopped

4 tbsps cooking oil

1 tsp ground turmeric

1 tsp ground coriander

1 tsp ground cumin

¼-½ tsp chilli powder

1 small tin of tomatoes

175ml/6fl oz warm water

2 cinnamon sticks, each 2-inches long;
   broken up

4 green cardamoms; split open the top of
   each pod

4 whole cloves

2 dried bay leaves, crumpled

1¼ tsp salt or to taste

2 level tbsps ghee or unsalted butter

1 large onion, finely sliced

1 tbsp chopped coriander leaves (optional)

---

1. Cut each chicken breast into 3 pieces. If you are using legs, separate leg from thigh.

Wash and dry on absorbent paper or a cloth.

2. Place the chopped onion, ginger and garlic into a liquidiser or food processor and liquidise to a smooth paste, add a little water, if necessary, to facilitate blade movement.

3. Heat the oil over medium heat and add the liquidised ingredients. Stir and fry for 4-5 minutes.

4. Add turmeric, coriander, cumin and chilli powder. Fry for 4-5 minutes stirring frequently. During this time, from the tin of tomatoes, add 1 tbsp juice at a time to prevent the spices from sticking to the pan. When you have used up all the tomato juice, add the chicken and fry it over medium-high heat until the chicken has changed colour.

5. Add the water, cinnamon, cardamom, cloves, bay leaves, salt and the whole tomatoes. Bring to the boil, cover and simmer until the chicken is tender and the gravy is fairly thick (about 25 minutes). Cook uncovered, if necessary, to thicken the gravy.

6. Heat the ghee or butter and fry the sliced onion for 5 minutes. Add the onions along with the ghee to the chicken. Remove from heat and stir in the coriander leaves.

TIME Preparation takes 15 minutes, cooking takes 45 minutes.

67

Classic Chicken Dishes

DAHI MURGHI

Dahi Murghi or chicken in yogurt needs little effort to cook and is simply gorgeous. The chicken is marinated in a yogurt-laced mixture and simmered until tender. Its simple method of cooking means that it can easily be fitted into a busy life style.

SERVES 4-6

1kg/2.2lbs chicken joints, skinned

125g/5oz carton of thick set natural yogurt

3-4 cloves garlic, peeled and coarsely chopped

1-inch cube of root ginger, peeled and coarsely chopped

2-3 dried red chillies

½ tsp ground turmeric

1 tbsp ground coriander

4 tbsps cooking oil

1 large onion, finely sliced

2-4 fresh green chillies, whole

1 tsp salt or to taste

½ tsp garam masala

2 tbsps chopped coriander leaves

1. Cut each chicken joint into two, separate leg from thigh and cut each breast into two pieces. Wash the chicken and dry on absorbent paper.

2. Put the yogurt, garlic, ginger, dried red chillies, turmeric and ground coriander in a liquidiser and blend until smooth.

3. Put the chicken in a large mixing bowl and pour the marinade over. Mix thoroughly, cover the container and leave to marinate for 6-8 hours, or overnight in the refrigerator.

4. Put the chicken into a heavy-based pan with a lid and place over medium heat, stirring occasionally until the chicken is heated through. Cover the pan and simmer gently until the chicken is tender (about 25-30 minutes). Remove the pan from heat.

5. Heat the oil over medium heat in a wide shallow pan and brown the onions.

6. Add the chicken and cook uncovered for 5-6 minutes stirring frequently.

7. Add the whole green chillies, salt and garam masala and cook for a further 3-4 minutes.

8. Remove the pan from the heat and stir in half the coriander leaves.

9. Put the chicken into a serving dish and sprinkle the remaining coriander leaves on top.

TIME Preparation takes 15 minutes plus time needed to marinate, cooking takes 30-35 minutes.

Classic Chicken Dishes

CHICKEN DHANSAK

Dhansak is a combination of two or three types of lentils and meat or chicken.

SERVES 6-8

1kg/2.2lbs chicken joints, skinned

1 tsp salt or to taste

1-inch cube of root ginger, peeled and coarsely chopped

4-6 cloves garlic, peeled and chopped

Grind the following 10 ingredients in a coffee grinder

1 tsp coriander seeds

1 tsp cumin seeds

1 tsp fennel seeds

4 green cardamoms

1 cinnamon stick, 2-inches long, broken up

4-6 dried red chillies

10 black peppercorns

2 bay leaves

¼ tsp fenugreek seeds

½ tsp black mustard seeds

2 tbsps ghee or unsalted butter

125ml/4fl oz warm water

For the dhal

75g/3oz toor dhal (yellow split peas)

75g/3oz masoor dhal (red split lentils)

5 tbsps cooking oil

1 large onion, finely chopped

1 tsp ground turmeric

1 tsp garam masala

600ml/20fl oz warm water

1 tsp salt or to taste

1 tsp tamarind concentrate (available from Indian grocers) or 1½ tbsp lemon juice

1 tbsp chopped coriander leaves, optional

---

1. Wash and dry the chicken portions and cut each portion into two.

2. Add the salt to the ginger and garlic and crush to a pulp.

3. Make a paste of the ground ingredients and the ginger/garlic pulp by adding 6 tbsps water. Pour this mixture over the chicken and mix to coat thoroughly. Cover and set aside for 4-6 hours or overnight in the refrigerator.

4. Melt the ghee or butter over medium heat and fry chicken for 6-8 minutes, stirring frequently. Add the water, bring to the boil, cover and simmer for 20 minutes. Stir several times.

5. Meanwhile, mix together the toor and masoor dhals, wash and drain well.

6. Heat the oil over medium flame and fry onions for 5 minutes, stirring frequently. Add turmeric and garam masala, stir and fry for 1 minute. Add the dhal, adjust heat to low and fry for 5 minutes, stirring frequently. Add the water and salt, bring to the boil, cover and simmer for 30 minutes until soft, stirring occasionally. Remove from heat.

7. Using a metal spoon, push some of the cooked dhal through a sieve until there is a very dry and coarse mixture left. Discard the coarse mixture and sieve the rest of the dhal the same way.

8. Pour the sieved dhal over the chicken, cover and place the pan over medium heat. Bring to the boil, reduce heat and simmer for 20-25 minutes. Stir occasionally during the first half of the cooking time, but more frequently during the latter half, to ensure that the mixture does not stick to the bottom of the pan.

9. Dissolve the tamarind pulp in 3 tbsps boiling water. Add this to the chicken/dhal mixture, stir and mix thoroughly. Cover and simmer for 5 minutes. Stir in the coriander leaves and remove from heat. If using lemon juice, simply add this at the end of the cooking time.

Classic Chicken Dishes

MURGH MUSALLAM
SERVES 4-6

2 spring chickens or poussin, each
    weighing about 450g/1lb

Grind together the following 5 ingredients
2 tbsps white poppy seeds
2 tbsps sesame seeds
10 black peppercorns
4 green cardamoms
2-4 dried red chillies

125g/5oz thick set natural yogurt
2½ tsps salt or to taste
½ tsp ground turmeric
1 tbsp ground coriander
75g/3oz ghee or unsalted butter
2 medium-sized onions, finely sliced
2-3 cloves garlic, peeled and finely
    chopped
2 cinnamon sticks, 2-inches each;
    broken up
6 green cardamoms, split open the top of
    each pod
4 whole cloves
275g/10oz basmati rice, washed and soaked
    in cold water for 30 minutes
570ml/20fl oz water
½ tsp saffron strands
2 tbsps ghee or unsalted butter
1 medium-sized onion, finely chopped
2-4 cloves garlic, peeled and crushed

---

1. Remove the skin and the giblets from the chicken. With a sharp knife, make several slits all over each chicken (do not forget the thighs and the back).
2. Mix the ground ingredients with the yogurt and add 1 tsp salt, turmeric and coriander. Rub half of this mixture into the chickens, making sure that the spices are rubbed deep into the slits. Put the chickens in a deep container, cover and keep aside for 1 hour.

3. Meanwhile cook the pilau rice. Melt the 75g/3oz ghee or butter over medium heat and fry the sliced onions, chopped garlic, cinnamon, cardamom and cloves, until the onions are lightly browned (6-7 minutes).
4. Add the rice, stir and fry until all the moisture evaporates (4-5 minutes). Add the remaining salt, water and saffron strands. Bring to the boil, cover the pan and simmer until the rice has absorbed all the water (12-14 minutes). Do not lift the lid or stir the rice during cooking. Remove the pan from the heat and leave it undisturbed for about 10 minutes.
5. Using a metal spoon, carefully transfer about a quarter of the cooked rice to a plate and allow it to cool. Keep the remaining rice covered.
6. Stuff each chicken with as much of the cooled pilau rice as the stomach cavity will hold. Truss it up as for roasting, using trussing needles or a similar object to secure it so that the rice stays in tact while the stuffed chicken is being braised.
7. Melt the 2 tbsps ghee or butter in a cast iron or nonstick pan. Add the chopped onions and the crushed garlic, stir and fry for 2-3 minutes.
8. Place the chicken on the bed of onions, on their backs, along with any marinade left in the container, but not the other half of the marinade which has been reserved. Cover the pan and cook for 10 minutes; turn the chicken over, breast side down, cover and cook for a further 10 minutes.
9. Turn the chickens on their backs again and spread the remaining marinade evenly on each chicken. Cover the pan and cook for 30 minutes turning the chicken over every 10 minutes.
10. Put the chicken onto a serving dish and spread a little gravy evenly over the breast. Spoon the remaining gravy round the chicken.
11. Serve the remaining pilau rice separately.

Classic Meat Dishes

ROGAN JOSH

Rogan Josh finds its origin in Kashmir, the northern-most state in India. In the recipe below, more than the usual quantity of spices are used, but these are toned down by using a large quantity of tomatoes and a little double cream.

SERVES 4-6

3 tbsps ghee or unsalted butter

1kg/2.2lbs leg of lamb, without bones, cut into 1½-inch cubes

1 tbsp ground cumin

1 tbsp ground coriander

1 tsp ground turmeric

1 tsp chilli powder

1-inch cube of root ginger, peeled and grated

2-4 cloves garlic, peeled and crushed

225g-275g/8-10oz onions, finely sliced

400g/14oz tin of tomatoes, chopped or whole

1 tbsp tomato purée

125ml/4fl oz warm water

1¼ tsps salt or to taste

90ml/3fl oz double cream

2 tsps garam masala

2 tbsps chopped coriander leaves

1. Melt 2 tbsps ghee or butter, from the specified amount, over medium heat and fry the meat in 2-3 batches until it changes colour. Remove each batch with a slotted spoon and keep aside.

2. Lower heat to minimum and add the cumin, coriander, turmeric, chilli powder, ginger and garlic. Stir and fry for 30 seconds.

3. Adjust heat to medium and add the meat along with all the ghee and juice in the container. Stir and fry for 3-4 minutes and add the onions. Fry for 5-6 minutes stirring frequently.

4. Now add the tomatoes and tomato purée – stir and cook for 2-3 minutes.

5. Add the water and salt, bring to the boil, cover and simmer until the meat is tender (about 60 minutes).

6. Stir in the cream and remove from heat.

7. In a separate pan melt the remaining ghee over medium heat and add the garam masala, stir briskly and add to the meat.

8. Transfer a little meat gravy to the pan in which the garam masala was fried – stir thoroughly to ensure that any remaining garam masala and ghee mixture is fully incorporated into the gravy and add this to the meat. Mix well.

9. Stir in the coriander leaves.

TIME Preparation takes 20 minutes, cooking takes 1 hour 30 minutes.

TO FREEZE Freeze before adding cream, garam masala and coriander leaves. Defrost thoroughly before reheating. Bring to the boil, add the cream and remove from heat. Add garam masala and coriander leaves.

VARIATION Use braising steak, but increase cooking time.

Classic Meat Dishes

Nawabi Kheema Pilau

*A rich rice dish in which mince is transformed into a wonderfully fragrant pilau
by the addition of saffron, rose water and fried nuts.*

SERVES 4-6

275g/10oz basmati rice
50g/2oz ghee or unsalted butter
1 tbsp extra ghee or unsalted butter
25g/1oz sultanas
25g/1oz raw cashews, split into halves
2 tbsps milk
1 tsp saffron strands
6 green cardamons, split open the top of
    each pod
4 whole cloves
1 tsp cumin seeds
2 bay leaves, crumpled
1-inch cube of root ginger, peeled and
    grated
2-3 cloves garlic, peeled and crushed
1-2 fresh green chillies, finely chopped and
    seeded if a milder flavour is preferred
1 tsp ground nutmeg
1 tsp ground cinnamon
1 tsp ground cumin
1 tbsp ground coriander
450g/1lb lean minced lamb
570ml/1 pint water
1½ tsps salt or to taste
150ml/5fl oz single cream
2 tbsps rosewater
2 hard-boiled eggs, sliced

1. Wash and soak basmati rice in cold water
for ½ hour, then drain.

2. Melt the 1 tbsp ghee or butter over low
heat and fry the sultanas until they swell up,
then remove with a slotted spoon and keep
aside.

3. In the same fat, fry the cashews until they
are lightly browned, remove with a slotted
spoon and keep aside.

4. Boil the milk, add the saffron strands and
put aside. Alternatively, put the milk and
the saffron strands in the microwave and
boil on full power or about 45 seconds. Set
aside.

5. Melt the remaining ghee or butter gently
over low heat and fry the cardamoms,
cloves, cumin seeds and the bay leaves for 1
minute.

6. Add the ginger, garlic and green chillies
and stir fry for 30 seconds.

7. Add all the nutmeg, ground cinnamon,
cumin and coriander and fry for 1 minute.

8. Add the mince and adjust heat to
medium. Stir and fry the mince until all
liquid dries up and it is lightly browned.
This will take about 5 minutes.

9. Add the rice, stir and fry for about 5
minutes.

10. Add the water, salt, cream and the
steeped saffron. Stir and mix well. Bring the
liquid to the boil, cover the pan and simmer
for 12-15 minutes without lifting the lid.
Remove the pan from the heat and keep it
undisturbed for a further 10-15 minutes.

11. Add half the nuts and raisins to the rice,
then sprinkle the rosewater evenly on top.
Using a fork, stir and mix in the ingredients
gently.

12. Put the pilau in a serving dish and
garnish with the remaining nuts and raisins
and the sliced hard-boiled eggs.

Time Preparation takes 20-25 minutes, cooking takes 40-45 minutes.

Classic Meat Dishes

MEAT MADRAS

This hot, but delicious curry is named after Madras, the major city in southern India, perhaps because in the humid south, people eat rather hot food. Strange though it may seem, this is because hot and spicy food makes one perspire, thereby cooling the body.

SERVES 4-6

6 tbsps cooking oil

2 medium-sized onions, coarsely chopped

1-inch cube of root ginger, peeled and coarsely chopped

3-4 cloves garlic, peeled and coarsely chopped

4-6 dried red chillies

2 large cloves garlic, peeled and crushed

1-2 fresh green chillies, sliced lengthwise

1 small tin of tomatoes

3 tsps ground cumin

1 tsp ground coriander

½-1 tsp chilli powder

1 tsp ground turmeric

1kg/2.2lbs leg or shoulder of lamb, fat removed and cut into 1½-inch cubes

175ml/6fl oz warm water

1¼ tsps salt or to taste

1 tsp garam masala

1. Heat 3 tbsps oil from the specified amount over medium heat and fry the onions, coarsely chopped ginger, garlic and red chillies until the onions are soft (8-10 minutes), stirring frequently. Remove from heat and allow to cool.

2. Meanwhile, heat the remaining oil over medium heat and fry the crushed garlic and green chillies until the garlic is lightly browned.

3. Add half the tomatoes, along with the juice; stir and cook for 1-2 minutes.

4. Add the cumin, coriander, chilli powder and turmeric, adjust heat to low and cook for 6-8 minutes, stirring frequently.

5. Add the meat and adjust heat to medium-high. Stir and fry until meat changes colour (5-6 minutes).

6. Add the water, bring to the boil, cover and simmer for 30 minutes.

7. Place the fried onion mixture in an electric blender or food processor and add the remaining tomatoes. Blend until smooth and add this to the meat – bring to the boil, add salt and mix well. Cover the pan and simmer for a further 35-40 minutes or until the meat is tender.

8. Stir in the garam masala and remove from heat.

TIME Preparation takes 25-30 minutes, cooking takes 1 hour 20 minutes.

Classic Meat Dishes

MEAT VINDALOO

Vindaloo is made by marinating the meat in vinegar and spices. It is traditionally a hot curry, but the quantity of chillies can be adjusted to suit individual taste.

SERVES 4-6

Grind the following 5 ingredients in a coffee grinder

2 tbsps coriander seeds

1 tbsp cumin seeds

6-8 dried red chillies

1 tbsps mustard seeds

½ tsp fenugreek seeds

3-4 tbsps cider or white wine vinegar

1 tsp ground turmeric

1-inch cube of root ginger, peeled and finely grated

3-4 cloves garlic, peeled and crushed

1kg/2.2lbs shoulder of lamb or stewing steak

4 tbsps cooking oil

1 large onion, finely chopped

1-2 tsps chilli powder

1 tsp paprika

1¼ tsps salt or to taste

450ml/15fl oz warm water

2-3 medium-sized potatoes

1 tbsp chopped coriander leaves, (optional)

---

1. In a large bowl, make a thick paste out of the ground spices, by adding the vinegar.

2. Add the turmeric, ginger and garlic. Mix thoroughly.

3. Trim off excess fat from the meat and cut into 1-inch cubes.

4. Add the meat and mix it well so that all the pieces are fully coated with the paste. Cover the bowl with cling film and leave to marinate for 4-6 hours or overnight in the refrigerator.

5. Put the meat in a pan and place this over medium heat, allow the meat to heat through, stirring occasionally; this will take about 5 minutes. Cover the pan, and cook the meat in its own juice for 15-20 minutes or until the liquid is reduced to a thick paste. Stir occasionally during this time to ensure that the meat does not stick to the bottom of the pan. Remove from heat and keep aside.

6. Heat the oil over medium heat and fry the onions until they are soft (about 5 minutes).

7. Add the meat and fry for 6-8 minutes stirring frequently.

8. Add the chilli powder, paprika and salt. Stir and fry for a further 2-3 minutes.

9. Add the water, bring to the boil, cover and simmer for 40-45 minutes or until the meat is nearly tender (beef will take longer to cook, check water level and add more water if necessary).

10. Meanwhile, peel and wash the potatoes. Cut them into approximately 1½-inch cubes. Add this to the meat and bring to the boil again. Cover the pan and simmer until the potatoes are cooked (15-20 minutes).

11. Turn the vindaloo on to a serving dish and sprinkle the coriander leaves on top.

TIME Preparation takes 10-15 minutes plus time needed for marinating, cooking takes 1 hour 30 minutes.

Classic Meat Dishes

MEAT DURBARI

The word 'Durbar' means forum or formal gathering. This wonderful lamb dish originated in the royal kitchens and was served at special gatherings held by the great Mughal Emperors.

SERVES 4

1kg/2.2lbs leg of lamb

Grind the following 9 ingredients in a coffee grinder and make a paste by adding the vinegar

1 tbsp mustard seeds

1 tbsp sesame seeds

2 tbsps white poppy seeds

10 black peppercorns

2-4 dried red chillies

1 bay leaf

2-inch piece of cinnamon stick, broken up

4 whole cloves

The inner seeds of 2 black cardamoms

3 tbsps white wine vinegar

1¼ tsp salt or to taste

3-4 cloves garlic, peeled and coarsely chopped

3 tbsps ghee or unsalted butter

1 large onion, finely chopped

1-inch cube of root ginger, peeled and finely grated

175ml/6fl oz warm water

1 tbsp tomato purée

2 fresh green chillies, slit lengthwise into halves, seeded for a milder flavour

2 tbsps chopped coriander leaves

1. Trim off excess fat from the meat and cut into 2-inch cubes.

2. Rub the spice paste well into the meat and leave to marinate for 4-6 hours, or overnight in the refrigerator.

3. Add the salt to the garlic and crush to a smooth pulp.

4. Melt the ghee or butter gently over low heat, add the onions and ginger, adjust heat to medium and fry them until the onions are soft (3-4 minutes).

5. Add the garlic paste and fry for a further 2-3 minutes stirring frequently.

6. Add the meat and cook in the onion mixture untill all sides of meat are sealed and brown.

7. Add the water, bring to the boil, cover and simmer until the meat is tender.

8. Add the tomato purée, green chillies and coriander leaves – adjust heat to medium and cook for 3-4 minutes stirring continuously. Remove the pan from the heat.

TIME Preparation takes 20-25 minutes plus time needed to marinate, cooking takes 1 hour 10 minutes.

Classic Meat Dishes

KOFTA (MEATBALL) CURRY

Koftas are popular throughout India, and they are made using fine lean mince which is blended with herbs and spices.

SERVES 4

For the koftas

450g/1lb lean minced lamb
2 cloves garlic, peeled and chopped
½-inch cube of root ginger, peeled and coarsely chopped
1 small onion, coarsely chopped
55ml/2fl oz water
1 fresh green chilli, seeded and chopped
2 tbsps chopped coriander leaves
1 tbsp fresh mint leaves, chopped
1 tsp salt or to taste

For the gravy

5 tbsps cooking oil
2 medium-sized onions, finely chopped
½-inch cube of root ginger, peeled and grated
2 cloves garlic, peeled and crushed
2 tsps ground coriander
1½ tsps ground cumin
½ tsp ground turmeric
¼-½ tsp chilli powder
1 small tin of tomatoes
150ml/5fl oz warm water
½ tsp salt or to taste
2 black cardamom pods, opened
4 whole cloves
2-inch piece of cinnamon stick, broken up
2 bay leaves, crumpled
2 tbsps thick set natural yogurt
2 tbsps ground almonds
1 tbsp chopped coriander leaves

1. Put half the mince, all the garlic, ginger, onion and the water into a saucepan and place over medium heat. Stir until the mince is heated through.

2. Cover and simmer until all liquid evaporates (30-35 minutes) then cook uncovered if necessary, to dry out excess liquid.

3. Combine the cooked mince with the rest of the ingredients, including the raw mince.

4. Put the mixture into a food processor or liquidiser and blend until smooth. Chill the mixture for 30 minutes.

5. Divide the mixture into approximately 20 balls, each slightly bigger than a walnut.

6. Rotate each ball between your palms to make neat round koftas.

7. Heat the oil over medium heat and fry the onions until they are just soft.

8. Add the ginger and garlic and fry for 1 minute.

9. Add the coriander, cumin, turmeric and chilli powder and stir quickly.

10. Add one tomato at a time, along with a little juice to the spice mixture, stirring until mixture begins to look dry.

11. Now add the water, salt, cardamom, cloves, cinnamon and the bay leaves.

12. Stir once and add the koftas. Bring to the boil, cover and simmer for 5 minutes.

13. Beat the yogurt with a fork until smooth, add the ground almonds and beat again – stir GENTLY into the curry. Cover and simmer until the koftas are firm.

14. Stir the curry GENTLY, cover again, and simmer for a further 10-15 minutes, stirring occasionally to ensure that the thickened gravy does not stick to the pan.

15. Stir in the coriander leaves and remove from heat.

Classic Meat Dishes

MEAT MAHARAJA

*A rich lamb curry cooked in the style favoured by the great Maharajas of India.
Ground poppy seeds and almonds are used to thicken the gravy and also to add
a nutty flavour.*

SERVES 4-6

---

4 tbsps ghee or unsalted butter

2 large onions, coarsely chopped

1-inch cube of root ginger, peeled and
    coarsely chopped

4-6 cloves garlic, peeled and coarsely
    chopped

1 fresh green chilli, seeded and chopped

1-2 dried red chillies, chopped

125g/5oz thick set natural yogurt

1 tsp black cumin seeds or caraway seeds

*Mix the following 4 ingredients in a small
bowl*

3 tsps ground coriander

1 tsp garam masala

1 tsp ground turmeric

¼ tsp ground black pepper

2 tbsps white poppy seeds, ground in a
    coffee grinder

1kg/2.2lbs leg of lamb, cut into 1-inch
    cubes

1¼ tsps salt or to taste

2 tbsps ground almonds

2 tbsps chopped coriander leaves

1 tbsp lemon juice

25g/2oz unsalted pistachio nuts, lightly
    crushed

1. Melt 2 tbsps ghee from the specified
amount over medium heat and fry the
onions, ginger, garlic, green and red chillies
until the onions are just soft (3-4 minutes).
Remove from heat and allow to cool
slightly.

2. Put the yogurt into an electric blender or
food processor, add the onion mixture and
blend to a purée. Keep aside.

3. Heat the remaining ghee or butter over
low heat (do not overheat ghee) and add
the black cumin or caraway seeds followed
by the spice mixture and the ground poppy
seeds. Stir and fry for 1 minute.

4. Add the meat, adjust heat to medium-
high, stir and fry until meat changes colour
(4-5 minutes). Cover the pan and let the
meat cook in its own juice for 15 minutes.
Stir occasionally during this time.

5. Add the blended ingredients and mix
thoroughly. Rinse out blender container
with 175ml/6fl oz warm water and add this
to the meat. Stir in the salt and bring the
liquid to the boil, cover the pan and simmer
until the meat is tender. Stir occasionally
during the first half of cooking time, but
more frequently towards the end to ensure
that the thickened gravy does not stick to
the bottom of the pan.

6. Stir in the ground almonds and half the
coriander leaves, cook, uncovered for 2-3
minutes.

7. Remove the pan from heat and add the
lemon juice, mix well. Garnish with the
remaining coriander leaves and sprinkle the
crushed pistachio nuts on top.

Classic Meat Dishes

ALOO GOSHT

A well-known north-Indian lamb curry with a distinctive flavour imparted by the ghee which is used to brown the potatoes before being added to the curry.

SERVES 4-6

1kg/2.2lbs leg or shoulder of lamb

1¼ tsps salt or to taste

1-inch cube of root ginger, peeled and coarsely chopped

3-4 cloves garlic, peeled and coarsely chopped

2 tbsps ghee or unsalted butter

450g/1lb medium-sized potatoes, peeled and cut into 1½-inch cubes

3 tbsps cooking oil

1 large onion, finely chopped

3-4 dried red chillies

2 cinnamon sticks, 2-inch long each, broken up

Make a paste of the following 5 spices by adding 3 tbsps water

1 tbsp ground coriander

1 tsp ground allspice

1 tsp paprika

1 tsp ground turmeric

¼-½ tsp chilli powder

1 tbsp tomato purée

2 black cardamoms, split open the top of each pod

4-6 whole cloves

450ml/15fl oz warm water

1 tbsp lemon juice

2 tbsps chopped coriander leaves

1. Trim off excess fat from the meat and cut it into 1½-inch cubes.

2. Add the salt to the ginger and garlic and crush to a pulp.

3. Melt the ghee or butter over medium heat in a non-stick or cast iron pan and fry the potatoes until they are well-browned on all sides (about 10 minutes). Remove the potatoes with a slotted spoon and keep aside.

4. Add the oil to any remaining ghee in the pan and when hot, fry the onions, red chillies and cinnamon sticks until the onions are soft (about 5 minutes).

5. Add the ginger and garlic pulp, and fry for a further 2-3 minutes stirring frequently.

6. Adjust heat to low and add the spice paste, stir and fry for 3-4 minutes.

7. Add the meat, adjust heat to medium-high, stir and fry until the meat changes colour (5-6 minutes), then stir in the tomato purée.

8. Now add the cardamoms, cloves and the water. Bring to the boil, cover and simmer for 45-50 minutes or 20 minutes in the pressure cooker with the 15lbs weight on.

9. Add the potatoes, bring to the boil again, cover and simmer for 15-20 minutes or until the potatoes are tender; if using pressure cooker, bring pressure down first, remove lid and add the potatoes. Cover and cook the potatoes without the weight.

10. Remove from heat and add the lemon juice and coriander leaves.

TIME Preparation takes 20-25 minutes, cooking takes 1 hour 30 minutes.

Classic Meat Dishes

SHAHI KORMA

The word 'Shahi' means royal, so the title itself is evidence that this particular korma was created in the royal kitchens of the great Maharajas of India. The dish is rich and creamy and is a perfect choice for a special occasion.

SERVES 4-6

1kg/2.2lbs boned leg of lamb, fat trimmed and cut into 1½-inch cubes

125g/5oz thick set natural yogurt

½-inch cube of root ginger, peeled and grated

3-4 cloves of garlic, peeled and crushed

50g/2oz ghee or unsalted butter

2 medium-sized onions, finely chopped

Grind the following ingredients in a coffee grinder

2 tbsps coriander seeds

8 green cardamoms with the skin on

10 whole black peppercorns

3-4 dried red chillies

Mix the following 2 spices with the above ground ingredients

1 tsp ground cinnamon

1 tsp ground mace

3-4 tbsps chopped fresh mint or 1½ tsps dried or bottled mint

50g/2oz ground almonds

300ml/10fl oz warm water

½ tsp saffron strands, crushed

1½ tsp salt or to taste

50g/2oz raw split cashews

150ml/5fl oz single cream

1 tbsp rosewater

1. Put the meat into a bowl and add the yogurt, ginger and garlic. Mix thoroughly, cover the bowl with cling film and leave to marinate for 2-4 hours or overnight in the refrigerator.

2. Put the marinated meat, along with any remaining marinade in the container, in a heavy-based saucepan and place it over medium-low heat. Bring to a slow simmer, cover and cook the meat in its own juice for 45-50 minutes stirring occasionally. Remove the pan from the heat and lift the meat with a slotted spoon. Transfer the meat to another container and keep hot.

3. Melt the ghee over medium heat and fry the onions until they are lightly browned (8-9 minutes).

4. Adjust heat to low and add the ground ingredients and the mint; stir and fry for 2-3 minutes. Add the half of the liquid in which the meat was cooked, stir and cook for 1-2 minutes. Add the ground almonds and mix thoroughly; add the remaining meat stock, stir and cook for a further 1-2 minutes.

5. Adjust heat to medium and add the meat, stir and fry the meat for 5-6 minutes.

6. Add the water, saffron strands, salt and cashews, bring the liquid to a slow boil, cover and simmer for 20 minutes.

7. Add the cream, stir and mix well, simmer uncovered for 6-8 minutes.

8. Stir in the rosewater and remove from the heat.

TIME Preparation takes 20-25 minutes, cooking takes 1 hour 30 minutes.

Classic Meat Dishes

KHEEMA SHAHZADA

Kheema, or mince is not at all an under-rated item in Indian cookery and in fact, the recipe below elevates mince to gourmet status. Do make sure that the mince is lean and that it is not too fine.

SERVES 4

4 heaped tbsps ghee or unsalted butter

1 large onion, coarsely chopped

1-inch cube of root ginger, peeled and coarsely chopped

2-4 cloves garlic, peeled and coarsely chopped

Grind the following ingredients in a coffee grinder

1 cinnamon stick, 2-inches long; broken up

4 green cardamoms

4 whole cloves

4-6 dried red chillies

1 tbsp coriander seeds

Grind the following 2 ingredients separately

1 tbsp white poppy seeds

1 tbsp sesame seeds

450g/1lb lean coarse mince

½ tsp ground turmeric

50g/2oz raw cashews, split into halves

1 tsp salt or to taste

300ml/10fl oz warm water

150ml/5fl oz milk

2 hard-boiled eggs, quartered lengthwise

A few sprigs of fresh coriander

1. Melt 2 tbsps ghee or butter from the specified amount, over medium heat and fry the onions, ginger and garlic until the onions are soft (about 5 minutes). Squeeze out excess fat by pressing the fried ingredients onto the side of the pan with a wooden spatula and transfer them to a plate. Allow to cool.

2. Add the remaining ghee or butter to the pan and fry the ground ingredients, including the poppy and sesame seeds, for 1 minute, stirring constantly.

3. Add the mince and fry until all the liquid evaporates (about 10 minutes), stirring frequently.

4. Add the turmeric, stir and fry for 30 seconds.

5. Add the salt, cashews and the water, bring to the boil, cover the pan and cook over low heat for 15 minutes, stirring occasionally.

6. Meanwhile, put the milk into an electric liquidiser followed by the fried onions, garlic and ginger. Blend until the ingredients are smooth and stir into the mince. Bring to the boil again, cover the pan and simmer for 10-15 minutes or until the gravy is thick.

7. Put the mince onto a serving dish and garnish with the hard-boiled eggs and the coriander leaves.

TIME Preparation takes 25-30 minutes, cooking takes 40-45 minutes.

Classic Meat Dishes

MEAT DILPASAND

A delectable lamb dish with a slightly creamy texture and a wonderfully nutty flavour derived from roasted and ground poppy seeds.

SERVES 4-6

1kg/2.2lbs leg of lamb
125g/5oz thick set natural yogurt
1 tsp ground turmeric
2 tbsps white poppy seeds
1-inch cube of root ginger, peeled and coarsely chopped
4-5 cloves garlic, peeled and coarsely chopped
1-2 fresh green chillies, seed them if a milder flavour is preferred
450g/1lb onions
3 tbsps ghee or unsalted butter
½ tsp chilli powder
1 tsp paprika
1 tbsp ground cumin
1 tsp garam masala
1 tbsp tomato purée
1¼ tsps salt or to taste
175ml/6fl oz warm water
25g/1oz creamed coconut or 2 tbsps desiccated coconut
2 tbsps chopped coriander leaves

1. Trim off any fat from the meat, wash and dry on absorbent paper and cut into 1½-inch cubes.

2. Add yogurt and turmeric, mix thoroughly, cover the container and leave to marinate for 4-6 hours or overnight in the refrigerator.

3. Roast the poppy seeds without fat over gentle heat until they are a shade darker – allow to cool.

4. Place the ginger, garlic and green chillies in an electric blender or food processor. Chop one onion, from the specified amount, and add to the ginger and garlic

mixture. Blend until fairly smooth.

5. Chop the remaining onions finely.

6. Melt the ghee or butter over medium heat and fry onions until golden brown. This will take 10 to 12 minutes.

7. Adjust heat to low and add chilli powder, paprika, cumin and ½ tsp garam masala from the specified amount. Stir and fry for 2-3 minutes.

8. Now add the liquidised ingredients and fry for 10 to 12 minutes, stirring frequently. If during this time the spices tend to stick to the bottom of the pan, sprinkle with about 1 tbsp of water at a time as and when necessary.

9. Add the meat and adjust heat to medium-high. Fry for 4-5 minutes stirring constantly.

10. Add the tomato purée, salt and water, stir and mix, bring to the boil, cover and simmer for 45 minutes or until the meat is tender. Stir occasionally during the first half of cooking, but more frequently towards the end to ensure that the thickened gravy does not stick to the bottom of the pan.

11. If you are using creamed coconut, cut into small pieces with a sharp knife. Desiccated coconut should be ground in the coffee grinder before use to ensure that the necessary fine texture is achieved in making the curry. Finish off the cooking process in the same way as for creamed coconut.

12. Grind the poppy seeds in a coffee grinder and stir into the meat along with the creamed coconut. Stir until coconut is dissolved. Cover and simmer for 15 minutes.

13. Stir in the coriander leaves and the remaining garam masala. Remove from heat.

Classic Meat Dishes

KHEEMA-PALAK (MINCE WITH SPINACH)

In India, mince is rarely cooked on its own. Various combinations are used to make it more interesting, and mince and spinach is one of the most popular.

SERVES 4-6

4 tbsps cooking oil

½ tsp black mustard seeds

1 tsp cumin seeds

1 fresh green chilli, finely chopped and seeded if a milder flavour is preferred

1-inch cube of root ginger, peeled and finely grated

6 cloves garlic, peeled and crushed

450g/1lb lean mince, lamb or beef

1 large onion, finely sliced

2 cinnamon sticks, 2-inches long each, broken up

½ tsp ground turmeric

1 tbsp ground cumin

½ tsp ground black pepper

325g/12oz fresh spinach leaves, chopped or 225g/8oz frozen spinach, defrosted and drained

1 tsp salt or to taste

1 small tin of tomatoes, drained and chopped or 3-4 medium sized ripe tomatoes, skinned and chopped

1 tsp garam masala

1. Heat half the oil in a wide shallow pan over medium heat and fry the mustard seeds until they crackle. Add the cumin seeds and immediately follow with the green chilli, ginger and half the garlic. Stir and fry for 30 seconds.

2. Add the mince, stir and fry until all the liquid evaporates – this will take 8-10 minutes. Remove the pan from the heat and keep aside.

3. In a separate pan, heat the remaining oil over medium heat and stir in the rest of the garlic. Add the onions and cinnamon sticks and fry until the onions are lightly browned (6-8 minutes), stirring frequently.

4. Adjust heat to low and add the turmeric, cumin and black pepper. Stir and fry for 1 minute. Add the spinach and mix thoroughly.

5. Add the mince and stir until the spinach and the mince are thoroughly mixed. Cover the pan and simmer for 15 minutes.

6. Adjust heat to medium, add salt and the tomatoes, stir and cook for 2-3 minutes.

7. Add the garam masala, stir and cook for a further 2-3 minutes. Remove the pan from heat.

TIME Preparation takes 15-20 minutes, cooking takes 40 minutes.

Classic Meat Dishes

PASANDA BADAM CURRY

Pasanda is a classic north Indian dish where the meat is cut into thin slices and cooked in a rich sauce containing saffron, yogurt and cream.

SERVES 4-6

900g/2lbs boned leg of lamb

1-inch cube of root ginger, peeled and coarsely chopped

4-6 cloves garlic, peeled and coarsely chopped

2 fresh green chillies, seeded and coarsely chopped

4 tbsps natural yogurt

50g/2oz ghee or unsalted butter

3 medium-sized onions, finely sliced

½ tsp ground turmeric

1 tsp ground cumin

2 tsps ground coriander

½ tsp ground nutmeg

¼-½ tsp chilli powder

225ml/8fl oz warm water

1¼ tsps salt or to taste

150ml/5fl oz single cream

25g/1oz ground almonds

1 tsp garam masala or ground mixed spice

2 tbsps rosewater

½ tsp paprika

1. Beat the meat with a meat mallet to flatten it to ¼-inch thickness, then cut into thin slices (about 1½-inch long and ½-inch wide).

2. Put the ginger, garlic, green chillies and yogurt into an electric liquidiser or food processor and blend until smooth.

3. Melt the ghee or butter over medium heat and fry the onions until they are lightly browned (6-8 minutes).

4. Add the turmeric, cumin, coriander, nutmeg and chilli powder; adjust heat to low, stir and fry for 2-3 minutes.

5. Add the meat and fry it over high heat for 3-4 minutes or until it changes colour.

6. Add about 2 tbsps of the liquidised ingredients and cook for 1-2 minutes, stirring frequently. Repeat this process until all the yogurt mixture is used up.

7. Now fry the meat over medium heat for 4-5 minutes stirring frequently. When the fat begins to seep through the thick spice paste and floats on the surface, add the water, bring to the boil, cover the pan and simmer until the meat is tender (about 60 minutes), stirring occasionally.

8. Add the salt, cream and ground almonds and let it simmer without the lid for 5-6 minutes.

9. Stir in the garam masala and rosewater and remove from heat.

10. Put the pasanda into a serving dish and sprinkle the paprika on top.

TIME Preparation takes 30 minutes, cooking takes 1 hour 20 minutes.

EGG & POTATO DUM

Hard-boiled curried eggs are very popular in the northeastern part of India. Here, the eggs are cooked with potatoes and they are both fried first until they form a light crust. Slow cooking, without any loss of steam, is the secret of the success of this dish.

SERVES 4-6

6 hard-boiled eggs
5 tbsps cooking oil
450g/1lb medium-sized potatoes, peeled and quartered
⅛ tsp each of chilli powder and ground turmeric, mixed together
1 large onion, finely chopped
½-inch cube of root ginger, peeled and grated
1 cinnamon stick, 2-inch long; broken up into 2-3 pieces
2 black cardamoms, split open the top of each pod
4 whole cloves
1 fresh green chilli, chopped
1 small tin of tomatoes
½ tsp ground turmeric
2 tsps ground coriander
1 tsp ground fennel
¼-½ tsp chilli powder (optional)
1 tsp salt or to taste
225ml/8fl oz warm water
1 tbsp chopped coriander leaves

1. Shell the eggs and make 4 slits lengthwise on each egg leaving about ½-inch gap on either end.

2. Heat the oil over medium heat in a cast iron or non-stick pan (enamel or steel pans will cause the eggs and the potatoes to stick). Fry the potatoes until they are well browned on all sides (about 10 minutes). Remove them with a slotted spoon and keep aside.

3. Remove the pan from heat and stir in the turmeric and chilli mixture. Place the pan back on heat and fry the whole eggs until they are well browned. Remove them with a slotted spoon and keep aside.

4. In the same oil, fry the onions, ginger, cinnamon, cardamom, cloves and green chilli until the onions are lightly browned (6-7 minutes).

5. Add half the tomatoes, stir and fry until the tomatoes break up (2-3 minutes).

6. Add the turmeric, ground coriander, fennel and chilli powder (if used); stir and fry for 3-4 minutes.

7. Add the rest of the tomatoes and fry for 4-5 minutes, stirring frequently.

8. Add the potatoes, salt and water, bring to the boil, cover the pan tightly and simmer until the potatoes are tender, stirring occasionally.

9. Now add the eggs and simmer, uncovered for 5-6 minutes, stirring once or twice.

10. Stir in the coriander leaves and remove from heat.

TIME Preparation takes 15 minutes, cooking takes 35-40 minutes.

Vegetarian Dishes

MIXED VEGETABLE CURRY

A variety of seasonal vegetables are cooked together in a gravy flavoured by a few ground spices, onions and tomatoes. Whole green chillies are added towards the end to enhance the flavour of the dish and also to retain their fresh green colour.

SERVES 4-6

4-5 tbsps cooking oil

1 large onion, finely chopped

½-inch cube of root ginger, peeled and finely sliced

1 tsp ground turmeric

1 tsp ground coriander

1 tsp ground cumin

1 tsp paprika

4 small ripe tomatoes, skinned and chopped or a small can of tomatoes with the juice

225g/8oz potatoes, peeled and diced

75g/3oz french beans or dwarf beans, sliced

100g/4oz carrots, scraped and sliced

75g/3oz garden peas, shelled weight

450ml/15fl oz warm water

2-4 whole fresh green chillies

1 tsp garam masala

1 tsp salt or to taste

1 tbsp chopped coriander leaves

1. Heat the oil over medium heat and fry the onions until they are lightly browned. (6-7 minutes).

2. Add the ginger and fry for 30 seconds.

3. Adjust heat to low and add the turmeric, coriander, cumin and paprika. Stir and mix well.

4. Add half the tomatoes and fry for 2 minutes, stirring continuously.

5. Add all the vegetables and the water. Stir and mix well. Bring to the boil, cover and simmer until vegetables are tender (15-20 minutes).

6. Add the remaining tomatoes and the green chillies. Cover and simmer for 5-6 minutes.

7. Add the garam masala and salt, mix well. Stir in half the coriander leaves and remove from heat.

8. Put the vegetable curry into a serving dish and sprinkle the remaining coriander leaves on top.

TIME Preparation takes 25-30 minutes, cooking takes 30 minutes.

TO FREEZE Suitable for freezing, but omit the potatoes. Add pre-boiled diced potatoes during reheating.

WATCHPOINT Frozen peas and beans may be used for convenience, but the cooking time should be adjusted accordingly. Cook the fresh vegetables first and follow cooking time for frozen vegetables as per instructions on packets.

Chapter 3
Side Dishes

KHUMBI AUR BESAN KI BHAJI

The use of mushrooms is somewhat limited in Indian cooking. However, in the West the abundant supply of mushrooms throughout the year makes it possible to create mouthwatering dishes at any time.

SERVES 4

325g/12oz white mushrooms
2 tbsps cooking oil
2-3 cloves garlic, peeled and crushed
½ tsp salt or to taste
½ tsp chilli powder
2 tbsps finely chopped coriander leaves
1 tbsp lemon juice
2 tbsps besan (gram flour or chick pea flour), sieved

1. Wash the mushrooms and chop them coarsely.

2. Heat the oil over medium heat and add the garlic. Allow garlic to turn slightly brown and add the mushrooms, stir and cook for 2 minutes.

3. Add salt, chilli powder and coriander leaves, stir and cook for 1 minute.

4. Add the lemon juice and mix well.

5. Sprinkle the besan over the mushroom mixture, stir and mix immediately. Remove from heat.

TIME Preparation takes 15 minutes, cooking takes 6-8 minutes.

SERVING IDEAS Serve as a side dish.
Suitable for freezing.

ALOO CHOLE

Chick peas are delicious cooked with spices and diced potatoes. They do need prolonged cooking before they are tender. If you have one it is worth cooking them in the pressure cooker which will only take 20 minutes with the 15lbs pressure on.

SERVES 4-6

225g/8oz chick peas, picked over and washed
900ml/30fl oz water
½-inch cube of root ginger, peeled and grated
1 large potato, peeled and cut into 1½-inch cubes
1 tsp ground cumin
½ tsp ground turmeric
¼-½ tsp chilli powder, optional
1-2 fresh green chillies, slit lengthwise into halves; seeded for a milder flavour
25g/1oz ghee or unsalted butter
1 large onion, finely chopped
1¼ tsp salt or to taste
½ tsp garam masala
1 tbsp lemon juice
1 tbsp chopped fresh mint or 1 tsp dried mint

1. Soak the chick peas overnight in plenty of cold water. Rinse several times and drain well.

2. Put the chick peas, water and ginger into a saucepan and place over a high heat, bring to the boil, cover the pan and simmer for 1¼-1½ hours or until the peas are tender. Alternatively, put the peas and the ginger in a pressure cooker and add 450ml/15fl oz water. Bring to the boil, then following the usual method for pressure cooking, cook under pressure for 20 minutes. Stand the pressure cooker aside until pressure is reduced.

3. Add the potatoes, cumin, turmeric, chilli powder and the green chillies, and the mint, if you are using it dried. Bring to the boil again, cover the pan and simmer for a further 15-20 minutes or until the potatoes are tender.

4. Melt the ghee over medium heat and fry the onions until they are lightly browned (6-8 minutes). Stir this into the chick peas along with the salt and garam masala.

5. Remove the pan from heat and stir in the lemon juice and fresh mint.

TIME Preparation takes 10-15 minutes plus time needed to soak the peas, cooking takes 1½-1¾ hours.

Mixed Vegetable Bhaji

In this delicious dish all the vegetables are cooked in a tightly covered dish in their own juice until tender, but firm. The dish has no gravy and is a perfect partner for most curries.

SERVES 4

---

3 tbsps cooking oil

½ tsp black mustard seeds

½ tsp cumin seeds

2-4 dried red chillies, whole

3-4 cloves garlic, peeled and crushed

¼-½ tsp chilli powder

100g/4oz carrots, scraped and cut into match stick strips

100g/4oz French beans or dwarf beans, cut to the same length as the carrots

225g/8oz potatoes, peeled and cut into matchstick strips

100g/4oz finely shredded onions

¾ tsp salt or to taste

15g/½oz fresh coriander leaves, including the tender stalks, finely chopped

1. Heat the oil in a wide shallow pan over medium heat.

2. Add the mustard seeds and as soon as they begin to pop, add the cumin seeds and the red chillies.

3. Add the garlic and chilli powder and immediately follow with all the vegetables and the onions.

4. Add the salt, stir and cook for 2-3 minutes. Cover the pan tightly and reduce heat to minimum setting. Let the vegetables sweat for 20-25 minutes, stirring occasionally.

5. Add the coriander leaves and stir-fry the vegetables over medium heat for 1-2 minutes and remove from the heat.

TIME Preparation takes 25 minutes, cooking takes 30 minutes.

SERVING IDEAS Serve with any meat/chicken/fish curry.

TO FREEZE Suitable for freezing, but as cooked potatoes do not freeze well, they should be omitted. Alternatively, add pre-boiled potatoes during re-heating.

Saag Bhaji

Spinach simmered in spices and combined with diced, fried potatoes.

SERVES 4-6

6 tbsps cooking oil

½ tsp black mustard seeds

1 tsp cumin seeds

8-10 fenugreek seeds (optional)

1 tbsp curry leaves

2-3 cloves garlic, peeled and finely chopped

2-4 dried red chillies, coarsely chopped

450g/1lb fresh leaf spinach or 225g/8oz frozen leaf spinach finely chopped

1 tbsp ghee or unsalted butter

1 large potato, peeled and diced

1 large onion, finely sliced

½ tsp ground turmeric

1 tsp ground cumin

½ tsp garam masala

¼-½ tsp chilli powder

2-3 ripe tomatoes, skinned and chopped

1 tsp salt or to taste

1. Heat 2 tbsps oil from the specified amount over medium heat and fry mustard seeds until they pop.

2. Add the cumin seeds, fenugreek (if used) and curry leaves and immediately follow with the garlic and red chillies. Allow garlic to turn slightly brown.

3. Add the spinach, stir and mix thoroughly. Cover and simmer for 15 minutes stirring occasionally.

4. Melt the ghee or butter over medium heat and brown the diced potatoes. Remove from heat and keep aside.

5. Heat the remaining oil over medium heat and fry onions until well browned (about 10 minutes), take care not to burn the onions or they will taste bitter.

6. Adjust heat to minimum and add turmeric, cumin, garam masala and chilli powder, stir and fry for 2-3 minutes.

7. Add the spinach, potatoes, tomatoes and salt, cover and simmer for 10 minutes or until the potatoes are tender, stirring occasionally. Remove from heat.

TIME Preparation takes 25-30 minutes, cooking takes 50 minutes.

POTATOES WITH GARLIC AND CHILLIES

*These are rather like spicy French fries, but they are not deep fried. A perfect
alternative to chips or French fries when you want a touch of spice with plain
meat, fish or chicken.*

SERVES 4-6

450g/1lb potatoes, peeled and washed
3 tbsps cooking oil
½ tsp black mustard seeds
½ tsp cumin seeds
4 cloves garlic, peeled and crushed
¼-½ tsp chilli powder
½ tsp ground turmeric
1 tsp salt or to taste

1. Cut the potatoes to the thickness of French fries, but half their length.

2. In a wide, shallow non-stick or cast iron pan, heat the oil over medium heat.

3. Add the mustard seeds and then the cumin. When the seeds start popping, add the garlic and allow it to turn lightly brown.

4. Remove the pan from the heat and add the chilli powder and turmeric.

5. Add the potatoes and place the pan back on heat. Stir and turn heat up to medium.

6. Add the salt, stir and mix, cover the pan and cook for 3-4 minutes and stir again. Continue to do this until the potatoes are cooked and lightly browned. Remove from the heat.

TIME Preparation takes 15-20 minutes, cooking takes 15 minutes.

SERVING IDEAS Serve with any curry and rice or Chapatties/Rotis.

VARIATION Use cauliflower florets, cut into small pieces.

KASHMIRI DUM ALOO

This is a lovely way to serve new potatoes. The potatoes are boiled, then fried until they are golden brown, and finally simmered gently in natural yogurt and spices.

SERVES 4

550g/1¼lbs small new potatoes
2 tbsps ghee or unsalted butter
1 tsp fennel seeds

Mix the following 5 ingredients in a small bowl
½ tsp ground cumin
1 tsp ground coriander
¼ tsp freshly ground black pepper
½ tsp ground turmeric
½ tsp ground ginger

125g/5oz thick set natural yogurt
1 tsp salt or to taste
¼ tsp garam masala
1 tbsp chopped coriander leaves
1 fresh green chilli, seeded and finely chopped

1. Boil the potatoes in their jackets, cool and peel them. Prick the potatoes all over with a tooth pick to enable the spices to penetrate deep inside.

2. Melt the ghee over medium heat in a non-stick or cast iron pan (steel or enamel pans will cause the potatoes to stick and break up).

3. When the ghee is hot, fry the potatoes in a single layer until they are well browned (8-10 minutes), turning them over frequently. Remove them with a slotted spoon and set aside.

4. Remove the pan from the heat and stir in the fennel seeds followed by the spice mixture. Adjust heat to low and place the pan back on the heat, stir the spices and fry for 1 minute.

5. Add the yogurt and salt, and mix well. Add the potatoes, cover the pan and simmer for 10-12 minutes. Add the garam masala and remove the pan from the heat.

6. Stir in the coriander leaves and the green chilli.

TIME Preparation takes 30-35 minutes including boiling the potatoes, cooking takes 20-25 minutes.

SPICY CHANNA DHAL

This is a speciality of the north-eastern region of India. In Assam and Bengal this dhal is invariably served during weddings and other special gatherings. Channa dhal is available from Indian grocers, but if it is difficult to get, yellow split peas can be used.

SERVES 4-6

225g/8oz channa dhal or yellow split peas

40g/1½oz ghee or unsalted butter

1 large onion, finely sliced

2 cinnamon sticks, each 2-inch long, broken up into 2-3 pieces

6 green cardamoms, split open the top of each pod

2-4 dried red chillies, coarsely chopped

½ tsp ground turmeric

¼-½ tsp chilli powder

1¼ tsps salt or to taste

600ml/20fl oz warm water

2 bay leaves, crumpled

40g/1½oz desiccated coconut

2 ripe tomatoes, skinned and chopped

2 tbsps chopped coriander leaves (optional)

1. Clean and wash the channa dahl or the yellow split peas and soak them for at least 2 hours. Drain well.

2. Melt the ghee or butter over medium heat and fry the onions, cinnamon, cardamom and red chillies until the onions are lightly browned (6-7 minutes).

3. Add the dhal, turmeric, chilli powder and salt. Stir-fry the dhal for 2-3 minutes. Adjust heat to low and fry the dhal for a further 3-4 minutes, stirring frequently.

4. Add the water, bay leaves, coconut and tomatoes. Bring to the boil, cover the pan and simmer for 35-40 minutes.

5. Stir in the coriander leaves (if used) and remove from the heat.

TIME Preparation takes 5-10 minutes plus time needed to soak the dhal, cooking takes 50-55 minutes.

TARKA DHAL
(SPICED LENTILS)

*Dhal of some sort is always cooked as part of a meal in an Indian household.
As a vast majority of the Indian population is vegetarian, dhal is a good
source of protein.*

SERVES 4

150g/6oz Masoor dhal (red split lentils)
750ml/1¼ pint water
1 tsp ground turmeric
1 tsp ground cumin
1 tsp salt or to taste
25g/1oz ghee or unsalted butter
1 medium-sized onion, finely chopped
2 cloves garlic, peeled and finely chopped
2 dried red chillies, coarsely chopped

---

1. Put the dhal, water, turmeric, cumin and salt into a saucepan and bring the liquid to the boil.

2. Reduce heat to medium and cook uncovered for 8-10 minutes, stirring frequently.

3. Now cover the pan and simmer for 30 minutes, stirring occasionally.

4. Remove the dhal from the heat, allow to cool slightly and mash through a sieve.

5. Melt the ghee or butter over medium heat and fry the onion, garlic and red chillies until the onions are well browned (8-10 minutes).

6. Stir in half the fried onion mixture to the dhal and put the dhal in a serving dish. Arrange the remaining fried onions on top.

TIME Preparation takes about 10 minutes, cooking takes about 50 minutes.

SERVING IDEAS Serve with Plain Boiled Rice and Murghi Jhal Frezi.

WATCHPOINT Pulses tend to froth and spill over. The initial cooking without the lid in stage 2 should help to eliminate this problem, but should you find that it is spilling over, then partially cover the pan until the froth settles down; this should take only a few minutes.

CABBAGE WITH CINNAMON

Cinnamon fried with onions has a rather distinctive and delicious flavour. The dish is not particularly spicy, but this combination gives it a special touch.

SERVES 4-6

---

4 tbsps cooking oil

1 large onion, finely sliced

2 fresh green chillies, sliced lengthwise; seeds removed if a milder flavour is preferred

3 cinnamon sticks, each 2-inches long; broken up into 2-3 pieces

1 large potato, peeled and cut into 1-inch cubes

½ tsp ground turmeric

¼ tsp chilli powder

125ml/4fl oz warm water

1 small white cabbage, finely shredded

1 tsp salt or to taste

1 tbsp chopped coriander leaves

1. Heat the oil over medium heat and fry the onions, green chillies and cinnamon sticks until the onions are soft (about 5 minutes).

2. Add the potatoes, stir and fry on low heat for 6-8 minutes.

3. Stir in the turmeric and chilli powder.

4. Add the water and bring it to the boil, cover the pan and simmer until the potatoes are half cooked (6-8 minutes).

5. Add the cabbage and salt, stir and mix well. Lower the heat to minimum setting, cover the pan and cook until the vegetables are tender (the cabbage should not be mushy). The finished dish should be fairly moist but not runny. If there is too much liquid left in the pan, take the lid off and let the liquid evaporate.

6. Stir in the coriander leaves and remove the pan from heat.

TIME Preparation takes 25 minutes, cooking takes 25 minutes.

TO FREEZE If you wish to freeze it, cook the cabbage only and add pre-boiled diced potatoes during reheating.

VARIATION For a colourful look, add 50g/2oz frozen garden peas.

CUCUMBER RAITA

*This raita is rather cooling and the aroma of the roasted cumin seeds
is very appetizing.*

SERVES 4-6

---

1 small cucumber
1 tsp cumin seeds
125g/5oz thick set natural yogurt
¼ tsp salt
¼ tsp paprika

---

1. Peel the cucumber and cut lengthwise into two halves. Slice each half finely.

2. Heat a small pan over low heat and dry roast the cumin seeds until they turn a shade darker. Allow the seeds to cool, then crush them with a rolling pin or pestle and mortar.

3. Beat the yogurt until smooth. Stir in the cumin along with the salt.

4. Reserve a few slices of cucumber for garnish and add the rest to the yogurt – mix thoroughly.

5. Put the raita into a serving dish and arrange the reserved cucumber on top.

6. Sprinkle the paprika evenly on the sliced cucumber.

TIME Preparation takes 15 minutes.

SERVING IDEAS Serve with Meat Vindaloo or Chicken Kohlapuri.

VARIATION Add half cucumber and half finely sliced radish.

TOMATO & CUCUMBER SALAD

*This salad, with its combination of cucumber, tomato and roasted peanuts
makes a mouthwatering side dish.*

SERVES 4-6

½ a cucumber

2 tomatoes

1 bunch spring onions, coarsely chopped

1 tbsp lemon juice

1 tbsp olive oil

¼ tsp salt

¼ tsp freshly ground black pepper

1 tbsp chopped coriander leaves

25g/1oz roasted salted peanuts, crushed

1. Peel the cucumber and chop finely.

2. Chop the tomatoes finely.

3. Put cucumber, tomatoes and spring onions into a serving bowl.

4. Combine the lemon juice, olive oil, salt, pepper and coriander leaves and keep aside.

5. Just before serving, stir in the peanuts and the dressing.

TIME Preparation takes 10 minutes.

SERVING IDEAS Serve with any meat, fish, chicken or vegetable curry.

VARIATION Omit the lemon juice and use 3 tbsps natural yogurt.

CABBAGE & MINT SALAD

An unusual touch is given to this salad by the bottled mint and natural yogurt used to coat the ingredients.

SERVES 4-6

275-325g/10-12oz white cabbage
1 small onion, finely chopped
1 fresh green chilli, finely chopped and
    seeded if a milder flavour is preferred
2-3 tbsps thick set natural yogurt
2 tsps mint sauce
½ tsp salt or to taste

1. Grate the cabbage (use the coarse side of a cheese grater or food processor) and put it into a large mixing bowl.

2. Add the rest of the ingredients and mix thoroughly.

3. Put the salad into a serving dish, cover and chill before serving.

TIME Preparation takes 10 minutes.

SERVING IDEAS Serve with Meat or Chicken Biriani, or rice and curry.

CARROT & PEANUT RAITA

A very tasty and easy to prepare side dish which has a high nutritional value.

SERVES 4-6

2 carrots

50g/2oz roasted salted peanuts

1 small clove of garlic, peeled and coarsely
    chopped

1 fresh green chilli, seeded and coarsely
    chopped

¼ tsp salt or to taste

125g/5oz thick set natural yogurt

½ tsp sugar

1 tbsp finely chopped coriander leaves
    (optional)

1. Peel and grate the carrots coarsely.

2. Crush peanuts with a wooden pestle or rolling pin.

3. Mix garlic, chilli and salt and crush to a pulp.

4. Beat the yogurt until smooth and stir in the garlic mixture.

5. Add the carrots, peanuts, sugar and coriander leaves (if using) and mix thoroughly.

TIME Preparation takes 10-15 minutes.

APPLE CHUTNEY

A mouthwatering relish with a sweet and sour, slightly hot flavour. Cooking apples are first tossed in a few spices and cooked until they are almost pulpy.

SERVES 8-10

1 tbsp cooking oil

½ tsp black mustard seeds

¼ tsp fenugreek seeds

¼ tsp ground turmeric

Pinch of asaphoetida

2 large cooking apples, peeled and finely
   chopped

½-¾ tsp chilli powder

1½ tsps salt or to taste

3 tbsps soft light brown sugar

1. Heat the oil over medium heat and fry the mustard seeds until they pop.

2. Add the fenugreek, turmeric and asaphoetida and immediately follow with the apples. Stir and mix thoroughly.

3. Add the chilli powder, salt and sugar, stir and cook until the apple starts secreting juice.

4. Cover and simmer until the apple is tender (5-6 minutes), stirring frequently.

5. Allow the chutney to cool and store in a moisture-free air-tight or screw-top jar. It can then be stored in the refrigerator for 4-6 weeks.

TIME Preparation takes 10 minutes, cooking takes 10 minutes.

SERVING IDEAS Serve with almost all snacks and starters.

CUMIN-CORIANDER CHUTNEY

The prominent flavour in this chutney is cumin, though equal quantities of cumin and coriander are used. Cumin has a stronger flavour than coriander and the mild and mellow coconut base in the chutney sets off the flavour beautifully.

SERVES 4-6

---

1 tsp cumin seeds

1 tsp coriander seeds

2-3 dried red chillies

4 tbsps desiccated coconut

55ml/2fl oz water

½ tsp salt or to taste

1½ tbsps lemon juice

2-3 tbsps finely chopped onions

1. Grind the cumin, coriander, red chillies and the coconut in a coffee grinder until the ingredients are smooth.

2. Transfer the ingredients to a bowl and add the water, salt and lemon juice. Mix thoroughly.

3. Stir in the onions.

TIME Preparation takes 10 minutes.

SERVING IDEAS Can be served with almost all fried snacks, or with rice and any meat, fish or vegetable curry. Suitable for freezing.

VARIATION Use ½ tsp tamarind concentrate dissolved in a little hot water instead of the lemon juice.

Chapter 4
Bread and Rice

CHAPATTIES

A Chapattie is a dry roasted unleavened bread best eaten as soon as it is cooked.
MAKES 14 Chapatties

325g/12oz fine wholemeal flour or Atta/
    Chapatti flour
½ tsp salt
1 tbsp butter, or ghee
170ml-280ml/6-10fl oz warm water
    (quantity depends on the texture of the
    flour)
1 tbsp extra flour in a shallow bowl or plate

---

1. Food Mixer Method: Place the flour, salt and fat together in the bowl and mix thoroughly at the medium-to-low speed taking care to see that all the fat has been broken up and well incorporated into the flour. Turn speed down to minimum and gradually add the water. When the dough is formed, knead it until it is soft and pliable. Cover the dough with a well-moistened cloth and keep aside for ½-1 hour.

2. Hand Method: Put the flour and salt in a large bowl and rub in the fat. Gradually add the water and keep mixing and kneading until a soft and pliable dough is formed. Cover the dough as above and keep aside.

3. Divide the dough into 14 walnut-sized portions. Roll each portion in a circular motion between the palms to make a smooth round ball, then flatten the ball to make a round cake. Dip each cake into the dry flour and roll the chapatti into a disc of about 6-inch diameter.

4. An iron griddle is normally used for cooking chapattis, but if you do not have one, then make sure you use a heavy-based frying pan as the chapatties need even distribution of heat during cooking. Overheating of the pan will cause the chapatties to stick to the pan and burn.

5. Heat the griddle or frying pan over medium heat and place a chapatti on it, cook for 30 seconds and turn the chapatti over. Cook until brown spots appear on both sides, turning it over frequently.

6. To keep the chapatties warm, line a piece of aluminium foil with absorbent paper and place the chapatties on one end, cover with the other end and seal the edges.

TIME Preparation takes 20-25 minutes, cooking takes 35-40 minutes.

SERVING IDEAS Serve with any meat, chicken or vegetable curry.
Suitable for freezing.

NAAN

Naan is traditionally cooked in the Tandoor. It is not difficult to cook naan in a very hot oven, although the distinctive taste of clay cooking will be missing.

MAKES 8 Naan

450g/1lb plain flour
1 tsp salt
1 tsp Kalonji-onion seeds, (optional)
1 tsp sugar
1½ sachets fast action or easy dissolve yeast
50ml/3fl oz milk
125g/5oz natural yogurt
1 medium-sized egg, beaten
50g/2oz ghee or butter
2 tbsps sesame seeds or white poppy seeds

1. Put the flour, salt, kalonji, sugar and yeast into a large bowl and mix well.

2. Warm the milk until it is lukewarm, reserve 1 tbsp yogurt and add the rest to the milk and blend thoroughly.

3. Beat the egg and keep aside.

4. Melt the butter or ghee.

5. Add the milk and yogurt mixture, egg and ghee or butter to the flour, knead with your hands or in the food processor or mixer until a soft and springy dough is formed.

6. Place the dough in a large plastic food bag and tie up the uppermost part so that the dough has enough room for expansion.

7. Rinse a bowl (preferably steel, as this will retain heat better) with hot water and put the bag of dough in it. Put the bowl in a warm place, until risen to double the original quantity (½-1 hour)

8. Divide the dough into 8 balls, cover them and keep aside for 10-15 minutes.

9. Preheat oven to 230°C/450°F/Gas Mark 8 and put an ungreased baking sheet into the over to preheat for about 10 minutes. Remove baking sheet from the oven and line with a greased greaseproof paper or baking parchment.

10. Take one of the balls and stretch it gently with both hands to make a teardrop shape. Lay this on the baking sheet and press it gently to stretch it to about 6-7-inches in length, maintaining the teardrop shape at all times. Make 2-3 similar shapes at a time and brush with the reserved yogurt, then sprinkle with the sesame or poppy seeds. Bake on the top rung of the oven for 10-12 minutes, or until puffed and browned.

TIME Preparation takes 10-15 minutes plus time needed to prove the dough, cooking takes 20-25 minutes.

SERVING IDEAS Serve with any meat, chicken or vegetable curry. Suitable for freezing.

VARIATION Use 1 tsp caraway or cumin seeds instead of the onion seeds while making the dough.

PURIS

This deep-fried unleavened bread is one of those items which needs last minute preparation. The dough can be made in advance, but rolling out and frying should be done simultaneously and once fried, they should be served immediately.

MAKES 14-15 Puris

275g/10oz fine wholemeal flour or atta or chapatti flour
½ tsp salt
¼ tsp sugar
1 tbsp margarine or oil
150-275ml/5-10fl oz warm water (quantity of water will depend on the texture of the flour – fine textured flour will absorb less water than the coarser variety)
Oil for deep frying

1. In a bowl, mix flour, salt and sugar. Rub in the margarine or oil. Now add the water very slowly and keep mixing and kneading until a stiff dough has formed. Alternatively, put the flour, salt, sugar and fat in a food processor or food mixer with a dough hook and switch on. When the fat is well incorporated into the flour, gradually add the water. Once the dough has been formed and kneaded for a few seconds, switch off the machine.

2. Divide the dough into 14-15 equal portions, each about 1½-inch diameter. Make the balls by rolling a portion of the dough between your palms in a circular motion. Have a little dry flour ready in a bowl or a plate. Dust each ball lightly in this and flatten the ball into a round cake. Treat all the balls the same way and cover them with a damp cloth.

3. Roll out the puris to about 3½-inch diameter discs. Rolling out should be done evenly to ensure tight edges which help the puris to puff up when they are dropped in hot oil. A flat perforated spoon is ideal for frying puris.

4. It is easier to roll and fry one puri at a time. If you wish to roll out all of them you will need a large work surface to keep them as they should not be piled together.

5. Careful handling is needed while rolling and frying the puris – if they are damaged or pierced, they will not puff up.

6. Heat the oil to 160°C in a deep fryer. Place one puri at a time in the oil and gently press it down – as soon as the puri puffs up turn it over and cook for about 30 seconds. Drain on absorbent paper. Fry the remaining puris in the same way.

7. Fried puris must not be heaped one on top of the other but placed on an open tray so as not to flatten or damage them (this stage is not important when the puris are made for the specific purpose of using with a filling).

TIME Preparation takes 5-10 minutes, cooking takes 15-20 minutes.

PLAIN BOILED RICE

Rice cookery needs no special technique, but a few simple rules will produce perfect results every time. Do not lift the lid while the rice is cooking. Do not stir the rice at any stage during cooking or immediately after it has been removed from the heat. This will ensure dry and separate grains every time.

SERVES 4-6

275g/10oz basmati or other long grain rice, washed and soaked in cold water for 30 minutes
1 tsp butter or ghee
½ tsp salt
500ml/18fl oz water

1. Drain the rice thoroughly and put into a saucepan with the water.

2. Bring to the boil, stir in the salt and the butter.

3. Place the lid on the saucepan and simmer: 12 minutes for basmati rice, 15 minutes for other long grain rice.

4. Remove from heat and keep the pot covered for a further 10-12 minutes.

5. Fork through the rice gently before serving. Use a metal serving spoon as wooden ones tend to squash the grains.

TIME Preparation takes 30 minutes, cooking takes 12-15 minutes.

SERVING IDEAS Plain Boiled Rice can be served with any curry. The rice can be garnished with fried onion rings or fresh coriander leaves.
Suitable for freezing.

PILAU RICE

Pilau is usually a beautifully fragrant rice or a combination of rice and meat, poultry, fish or vegetables. It is always cooked in pure butterfat ghee, but unsalted butter is a good substitute.

SERVES 4-6

275g/10oz basmati rice
50g/2oz ghee or unsalted butter
1 large onion, finely sliced
2-4 cloves garlic, peeled and finely chopped
8 whole cloves
8 green cardamoms, split open the top of each pod
2 cinnamon sticks, 2-inches long each, broken up
8 whole peppercorns
1 tsp ground turmeric
570ml/20fl oz water
1¼ tsps salt or to taste
1 heaped tsp butter
25g/1oz seedless sultanas
25g/1oz flaked almonds

1. Wash the rice and soak in cold water for ½ an hour. Drain well.

2. In a heavy-based pan melt the ghee or butter over medium heat and fry onions until they are soft but not brown (about 5 minutes).

3. Add the garlic, cloves, cardamoms, cinnamon sticks and peppercorns. Stir and fry until the onions are golden brown (3-4 minutes).

4. Add the rice and turmeric, stir and fry for 1-2 minutes. Adjust heat to low, stir and fry the rice for a further 2-3 minutes.

5. Add the water and the salt, bring to the boil, cover and simmer for 15 minutes without lifting the lid.

6. Remove the pan from heat and keep it undisturbed for a further 10-12 minutes.

7. Melt the 1 tsp butter over gentle heat and fry sultanas until they change colour and swell up (1 minute). Transfer the sultanas onto a plate and in the same fat fry the almonds until they are lightly browned. Remove and put onto a separate plate.

8. Put the pilau rice into a serving dish and, using a fork, gently mix in the fried sultanas and almonds.

TIME Preparation takes 10 minutes plus time needed to soak the rice, cooking takes 25-30 minutes.

FRIED BROWN RICE

This is the traditional rice dish which accompanies chicken or meat dhansak. It can also be served with a host of other dishes.

SERVES 4-6

275g/10oz basmati or other long grain rice
4 tbsps cooking oil
4 tsps sugar
1 tsp cumin seeds
2 cinnamon sticks, 2-inches long each,
    broken up
6 whole cloves
6 black peppercorns
2 bay leaves, crumpled
570ml/20fl oz water
1 tsp salt

1. Wash the rice and soak in cold water for 30 minutes. Drain well.

2. In a heavy-based saucepan, heat the oil over medium heat and add the sugar.

3. The sugar will gradually begin to change colour to a dark brown. As soon as it does, add the cumin seeds, cinnamon, cloves, black peppercorns and bay leaves. Fry for 30 seconds.

4. Add the rice and fry for about 5 minutes, stirring frequently and lowering heat towards the last minute or two.

5. Add the water and salt. Bring to the boil, cover and simmer without lifting the lid: 12-15 minutes for basmati rice, 15-18 minutes for other long grain rice.

6. Remove the pan from heat and keep it undisturbed for a further 10-15 minutes before serving.

TIME Preparation takes a few minutes plus time needed to soak the rice, cooking takes 20-25 minutes.

WATCHPOINT If the lid is lifted and the rice is stirred during cooking, the loss of steam will cause the rice to stick and turn soggy. Do not handle the rice immediately after it has been cooked to ensure dry and separate grains.

CARROT PILAU

An imaginative way to turn plain boiled rice, left over or freshly cooked, into a colourful and flavoursome pilau which can be served with meat, fish or chicken curry.

SERVES 4-6

275g/10oz basmati rice, washed and soaked in cold water for ½ hour
500ml/18fl oz water
1 tsp salt or to taste
1 tsp butter or ghee
2 tbsps ghee or unsalted butter
1 tsp cumin or caraway seeds
1 medium-sized onion, finely sliced
2 cinnamon sticks, each 2-inches long, broken up
4 green cardamoms, split open the top of each pod
1 tsp garam masala or ground mixed spice
150g/6oz coarsely grated carrots
100g/4oz frozen garden peas
½ tsp salt or to taste

1. Drain the rice thoroughly and put into a saucepan with the water.

2. Bring to the boil, stir in the salt and the butter.

3. Allow to boil steadily for 1 minute.

4. Place the lid on the saucepan and simmer for 12-15 minutes. Do not lift the lid during this time.

5. Remove the pan from heat and keep it covered for a further 10 minutes.

6. Meanwhile, prepare the rest of the ingredients.

7. Melt the ghee or butter over medium heat and fry cumin or caraway until they crackle.

8. Add the onions, cinnamon and cardamom. Fry until the onions are lightly browned (4-5 minutes), stirring frequently.

9. Add the garam masala or ground mixed spice, stir and cook for 30 seconds.

10. Add the carrots, peas and the salt, stir and cook for 1-2 minutes.

11. Now add the rice, stir and mix gently using a metal spoon or a fork as wooden spoon or spatula will squash the grains. Remove the pan from heat.

TIME Preparation takes 10-15 minutes plus time needed to soak the rice, cooking takes 25-30 minutes.

Chapter 5
Drinks and Desserts

MANGO SHERBET

Mango Sherbet is a delicious and nourishing drink. The quantities used here make a thick sherbet which can be thinned down by adding more milk or water as desired.

MAKES 2 pints

1 × 450g/1lb can of mango pulp
or 2 × 425g/15oz cans of sliced mangoes,
    drained
570ml/20fl oz milk
4 tbsps caster sugar
1 tsp ground cardamom
1 tbsp rosewater (optional)
300ml/10fl oz cold water

1. Put the mango pulp or slices, half the milk, sugar, cardamom and rosewater into an electric liquidiser or food processor and switch on for a few seconds.

2. Transfer the contents into a large jug or bowl and add the remaining milk and the water.

3. Chill for 2-3 hours.

TIME Preparation takes a few minutes.

SERVING IDEAS Serve during meals or at a barbecue.

VARIATION Omit the milk and use all water. Top the drink with a scoop of vanilla ice cream.

SPICY PINEAPPLE PUNCH

A lovely drink to welcome your guests; serve it warm before lunch, especially at Christmas time, or enjoy it chilled with your barbecue during the long, warm summer evenings.

SERVES 6-8

450ml/15fl oz water

1 litre/36fl oz carton of pineapple juice

5 cinnamon sticks, each 2-inches long; broken up

12 whole cloves

12 green cardamoms, bruised

15g/½oz fresh mint leaves, chopped

175ml/6fl oz brandy

1. Put the water, half the pineapple juice, cinnamon, cloves, cardamom and mint into a saucepan. Bring to the boil, cover the pan and simmer gently for 20 minutes.

2. Remove from the heat and allow to cool. Keep the pan covered.

3. Strain the drink and add the remaining pineapple juice and the brandy. Mix well.

TIME Preparation takes 5 minutes, cooking takes 20-25 minutes.

KULFI (INDIAN ICE CREAM)

Kulfi is by far the most popular ice cream in India. It is firmer than conventional ice cream and is usually set in small tin or aluminium moulds. You can, however, use either small yogurt pots or a plastic ice cream box.

SERVES 6-8

150ml/5fl oz fresh milk
2 tbsps ground rice
1 tbsp ground almonds
450ml/14½oz tin evaporated milk
1 level tsp ground cardamom
50g/2oz sugar
450ml/15fl oz double cream
1 tbsp rose water or 5-6 drops of any other
    flavouring such as vanilla, almond etc.
25g/1oz shelled, unsalted pistachio nuts,
    lightly crushed

---

1. Heat the milk until it is lukewarm.

2. Put the ground rice and ground almonds into a small bowl and gradually add the warm milk, a little at a time, and make a thin paste of pouring consistency. Stir continuously and break up any lumps, if any lumps remain, sieve the paste.

3. Heat evaporated milk to boiling point and add the ground cardamom.

4. Take the pan off the heat and gradually add the almond/rice mixture, stirring continuously.

5. Add the sugar and cream and place the pan over medium heat, cook the mixture for 12-15 minutes, stirring continuously. Remove the pan from heat and allow the mixture to cool slightly.

6. Add the rosewater flavouring and half of the pistachio nuts, stir and mix well. Allow the mixture to cool completely, stirring frequently to prevent a skin from forming on the surface.

7. When the mixture has cooled completely, put it into a plastic ice cream box or individual moulds.

8. Top with the remaining pistachio nuts and place in the freezer or in the ice-making compartment of a refrigerator for 4-5 hours.

9. Place the kulfi in the refrigerator for 1½-1 ¾ hours before serving. This will soften the kulfi slightly and will make it easier to cut into desired size when it is set in an ice cream box. The time required to soften the kulfi will vary according to the size of the container used.

TIME Preparation takes 10 minutes, cooking takes 15-20 minutes.

DURBARI MALPURA

A great delicacy from the courts of the Mughal Emperors, these small pancakes are smothered with dried fruits and nuts and cream, and delicately flavoured with nutmeg and orange rind.

SERVES 6

75g/3oz plain flour
25g/1oz ground rice
50g/2oz caster sugar
1 tsp ground or finely grated nutmeg
Pinch of bicarbonate of soda
Finely grated rind of 1 orange
25g/1oz each of raw cashews and walnuts, lightly crushed
125ml/4fl oz full cream milk
Oil for deep frying
1 tsp butter
25g/1oz sultanas
25g/1oz flaked almonds
300ml/10fl oz single cream
1 tbsp rose water

1. Put the flour, ground rice, sugar, nutmeg, soda bicarbonate, orange rind and the crushed nuts into bowl.

2. Add the milk and stir until a thick batter is formed.

3. Heat the oil over medium heat in a deep frying pan.

4. Put in 1 heaped teaspoon of the batter at a time until the whole pan is filled with a single layer.

5. When the malpuras (spoonfuls of batter) start floating to the surface, turn them over. Fry gently until golden brown on both sides (about 5 minutes). Drain on absorbent paper.

6. Melt the butter over low heat and fry the sultanas for 1 minute. Remove them with a slotted spoon and drain on absorbent paper.

7. In the same fat, fry the almonds until they are lightly browned. Drain on absorbent paper.

8. Put the cream in a saucepan, large enough to hold all the malpuras and bring to a slow simmer.

9. Put in the malpuras and stir gently.

10. Turn the entire contents of the pan onto a serving dish and sprinkle the rosewater evenly on top.

11. Garnish with the fried sultanas and the almonds. Serve hot or cold.

TIME Preparation takes 10 minutes, cooking takes 20 minutes.

VARIATION Use lemon rind instead of orange.

COCONUT STUFFED PANCAKES

Coconut is used for both sweet and savoury dishes in southern India. There is no substitute for freshly grated coconut, but as it is quite time consuming, desiccated coconut is a good compromise.

MAKES 6 pancakes

For the filling

50g/2oz desiccated coconut
50g/2oz soft dark brown sugar
25g/1oz walnut pieces, lightly crushed
1 small tin evaporated milk
1 tsp ground cardamom

1. Mix all ingredients, except ground cardamom, in a small saucepan and place over medium heat. As soon as it begins to bubble, reduce heat to low and let it simmer without a lid for 8-10 minutes stirring occasionally.

2. Stir in the ground cardamom, remove the pan from heat and allow the mixture to cool.

For the pancakes

2 eggs
150g/6oz wholemeal flour
1 tsp ground cinnamon
1 tbsp caster sugar
200ml/7fl oz milk
Ghee or unsalted butter for frying

1. Put all ingredients, except ghee or butter, in a large bowl and beat with a wire beater until smooth. This batter can also be prepared in a liquidiser or food processor.

2. Place a non-stick or cast iron frying pan over low heat, when hot, spread a little (about ¼ tsp) ghee or butter on it.

3. Pour about 2 tbsps of the batter in the pan and spread it quickly by tilting the pan. Pouring off the batter must be done quickly in one go to prevent it from setting before you have a chance to spread it. It is easier to measure each 2 tbsps into a cup or a small bowl before pouring into the pan.

4. In a minute or so, the pancake will set, let it cook for a further minute, then carefully turn it over with a thin spatula or toss it! Cook the other side for about 1 minute (brown spots should appear on both sides).

5. Spread 1 tbsp of the stuffing on one side of the pancake and roll it into a cylinder shape. Make the rest of the pancakes the same way.

TIME Preparation takes 15-20 minutes, cooking takes 50 minutes.

SERVING IDEAS Serve on their own as a tea-time snack or topped with a little whipped cream as a dessert.

WATCHPOINT Use a wide, thin spatula to turn the pancakes; wooden spatulas are too thick and they will squash the pancakes. Steel or plastic slotted spatulas are ideal.

FIRNI (CREAMED GROUND RICE WITH DRIED FRUIT AND NUTS)

Although firni is basically a rice pudding, it is a far cry from the western creamed rice or rice pudding. Firni is rich, delicious and temptingly aromatic.

SERVES 6-8

300ml/10fl oz fresh milk
45g/1½oz ground rice
1 tbsp ground almonds
500g/14oz tin of evaporated milk
50g/2oz sugar
1 tbsp rosewater
1 tsp ground cardamom
25g/1oz flaked almonds
25g/1oz pistachio nuts, lightly crushed
25g/1oz dried apricot, finely chopped

1. Put the fresh milk into a heavy-based saucepan over a medium heat.

2. Mix the ground rice and ground almonds together and sprinkle evenly over the milk.

Bring the milk to the boil, stirring frequently.

3. Add the evaporated milk and sugar, stir and cook over a low heat for 6-8 minutes.

4. Remove from heat and allow the mixture to cool – stirring occasionally to prevent skin from forming on top.

5. Stir in the rosewater and the ground cardamom.

6. Reserve a few almonds, pistachios and apricots and stir the remainder into the pudding.

7. Transfer the firni into a serving dish and top with the reserved fruit and nuts. Serve hot or cold.

TIME Preparation takes 5-10 minutes, cooking takes about 15 minutes.

VARIATION Add a few raw cashews (coarsely chopped) while cooking the ground rice and ground almonds.

SHRIKAND

Shrikand is a delicious and creamy dessert which is made of strained yogurt. The yogurt is tied and hung until all the water content has drained off, the result being a thick and creamy yogurt which is rich but delicious.

SERVES 6

3 × 425g/15oz cartons of thick set natural
   yogurt
¼ tsp saffron strands
1 tbsp hot water
75g/3oz caster sugar
1 heaped tbsp ground almonds
½ tsp ground cardamom
¼ tsp grated or ground nutmeg

1. Pour the yogurt onto a clean, very fine muslin cloth; bring together the four corners of the cloth so that the yogurt is held in the middle. Tie the four corners into a tight knot and hang the muslin over the sink until all the water content has been drained off; 4-6 hours or undisturbed overnight.

2. Add the saffron strands to the hot water, cover and keep aside.

3. Untie the muslin cloth carefully and empty the contents into a mixing bowl. Beat the strained yogurt with a fork, or a wire beater, until smooth.

4. Add the sugar, beat and mix thoroughly. Add the ground almonds, cardamom and the nutmeg and mix well.

5. Stir in the saffron strands and the water in which it was soaked.

6. Chill before serving.

TIME Preparation takes a few minutes plus time needed to drain the yogurt.

VARIATION Top the Shrikand with mandarin orange segments, sliced mangoes or chopped pistachio nuts.

SPICED FRUIT SALAD

A novel deviation from traditional Indian desserts, but an excellent one to round off an Indian meal. Handle the tinned mango slices very carefully as they tend to be far too soft. Use fresh mangoes instead if you have a friendly bank manager!

SERVES 6-8

425g/15oz tin pineapple chunks
425g/15oz tin papaya (paw paw) chunks
425g/15oz tin mango slices, cut into chunks
425g/15oz tin guava halves, cut into chunks
3 cinnamon sticks, each 2-inches long
3 black cardamoms
6 whole cloves
8 black peppercorns

1. Drain all the fruits and reserve the syrup. Mix all the syrup together, reserve 570ml/20fl oz and drain off remainder.

2. Put the syrup into a saucepan and add the spices, bring to the boil, cover the pan and let it simmer for 20 minutes.

3. Uncover and reduce the syrup to half its original volume by boiling for 5-6 minutes. Remove from heat and allow the syrup to cool.

4. Keep the pan covered until the syrup cools, (in an open pan some of the flavour will be lost).

5. Reserve a few pieces of papaya and guava and all the mangoes. Arrange the remaining fruits in a serving bowl.

6. Arrange the mangoes on top, then put in the reserved papaya and guava.

7. Strain the spiced syrup and pour over the fruits. Cover with cling film and chill.

TIME Preparation takes 10-15 minutes, cooking takes 20 minutes.

VARIATION Use fresh ripe William pear instead of tinned mango. Add 1 tbsp of brandy to the syrup.

VERMICELLI KHEER

In this popular pudding, the vermicelli is first lightly fried in ghee, then simmered gently in milk with sugar and spices to make a rich and creamy dish.

SERVES 6-8

2 tbsps ghee or unsalted butter
25g/1oz plain vermicelli
25g/1oz sultanas
25g/1oz almonds, blanched and slivered
570ml/20fl oz full cream milk
50g/2oz sugar
1 tbsp ground almonds
½ tsp ground cardamom
½ tsp ground cinnamon
1 tbsp rose water or 5-6 drops of other
   flavourings such as vanilla or almond

1. Melt the ghee or butter over low heat and add the vermicelli, sultanas and slivered almonds. Stir and fry until the vermicelli is golden brown (2-3 minutes).

2. Add the milk, sugar and ground almonds, bring to the boil and simmer gently for 20 minutes, stirring frequently.

3. Stir in the ground cardamom and cinnamon and remove the pan from heat.

4. Allow the kheer to cool slightly and stir in the rose water or other flavouring.

TIME Preparation takes 10 minutes, cooking takes 20-25 minutes.

SERVING IDEAS Serve hot or cold.

Index